CW01261257

BOUNCEBACK FOOD

Secret Dishes From Around the World 2

£25.00

First published in 2020 by Bounceback Books
2 Federation Street
Manchester
M4 4BF
info@bouncebackfood.co.uk
www.bouncebackfood.co.uk

ISBN: 978-1-9162650-3-5

Text: Copyright © Duncan Swainsbury
Artwork: Copyright © Jack Whitelegg © Natalija Stolarova © Bernice Tackley © Sam Tomson © Michael Wylie © Tommy Bradley © Lydia Fernandez-Arias © Victoria Rebekah © Emma Reynolds © James Blinkhorn © Alexandra Boocock © Peter Lang © Jessica Owen © Rory Spencer © Jamie Griffiths © Christian Turner © Holly Gorne © Emily Gibbs © Amberley Garland © Ollie Hirst
Photographs: Copyright © Bounceback Food CIC
Graphic design by Peter Lang.
Printed in Turkey. Production managed by Jellyfish Solutions.

Duncan Swainsbury has asserted his right under the Copyright, Designs and Patents Act 1988 to be identified as the author of this work. All rights reserved. No part of this publication may be reproduced, stored in a retrieval system or transmitted in any form, or by any means (electronic, mechanical, or otherwise) without the prior written permission of Bounceback Books.

All proceeds from the sale of this book will help fund future Bounceback Food CIC projects.

A CIP catalogue record of this book is available from the British Library.

SECRET DISHES
FROM AROUND THE WORLD
2

Acknowledgements

This book is dedicated to all of the members of our community cookery school. Without their support, especially during this turbulent year, we wouldn't have been able to scale up our social impact and proactive fight against food poverty.

We also couldn't have written this sequel without support from the 20 talented artists who were selected to represent Greater Manchester, Cheshire and North Wales, the areas where Bounceback Food CIC delivers outreach work. They were instrumental in the success of our crowdfunding campaign and their artwork is truly magnificent!

Special mention must also go to:

DSH CABLES & CONTROLS

Our first corporate sponsor who decided to 'Back the Book' and get behind the development of our Cooking & Nutrition Portal.

Social Enterprise UK

Thank you for promoting our social enterprise and raising the profile of our sector on a national scale.

school for social entrepreneurs

Thank you for guiding the development of our organisation with your superb Start Up, Trade Up and Scale Up Learning Programmes!

Thank you to our partner cookery workshop venues and foodbank collection points for supporting our proactive fight against food poverty from day 1.

Design Credits

WE WOULD ALSO LIKE TO THANK

Peter Lang

Peter is an experienced freelance graphic designer with over 10 years experience working in and around Greater Manchester.

For a second time he has helped us to create a stunning recipe book that combines art, photography and exciting recipes from around the world!

Discover more of his work at:

www.peterdoesdesign.co.uk

Josh Rea

Josh is our multi-talented head chef who developed our secret dishes and also took the beautiful photographs that accompany each recipe!

He studied Photography at Manchester Metropolitan University and joined Bounceback Food CIC via our annual internship programme back in 2018.

Find out more at:

www.bouncebackfood.co.uk/internships

20 Countries. 20 Artists.

Secret Dishes From Around the World 2!

Thank you for purchasing a copy of our second fundraising recipe book, *Secret Dishes From Around the World 2!*

In doing so, you're supporting the development of our community cookery school as we continue to fight food poverty proactively across Greater Manchester, Cheshire and North Wales. Since 2014, we've used the **buy one, give one** model to teach 2,000+ people how to cook, donate 10,000+ items of food to foodbanks and provide 75,000+ meals as part of our wider community outreach work which includes catering, supper clubs and corporate cook offs!

You're also supporting the 20 talented artists who, inspired by the countries and recipes, each produced an original piece of art. You can discover their designs in the book and find out more about their work in the 'Meet the Artists' section that begins on page 16.

In a year where we've all been forced to spend time apart it's heart-warming to know that creativity, collaboration and community spirit have prevailed. We hope that you enjoy making our second collection of *Secret Dishes From Around the World!*

Happy cooking,

The Bounceback Team

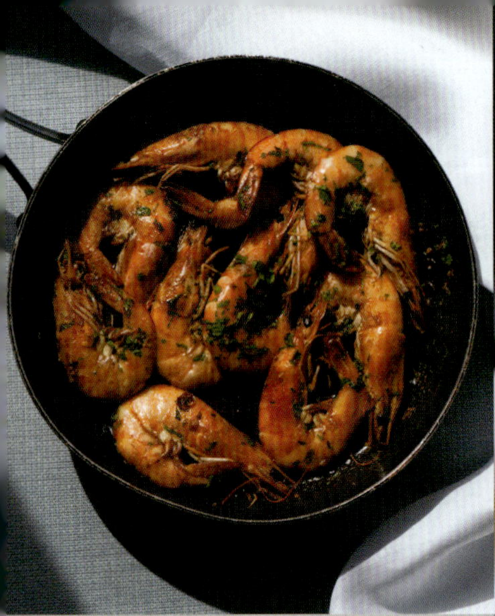
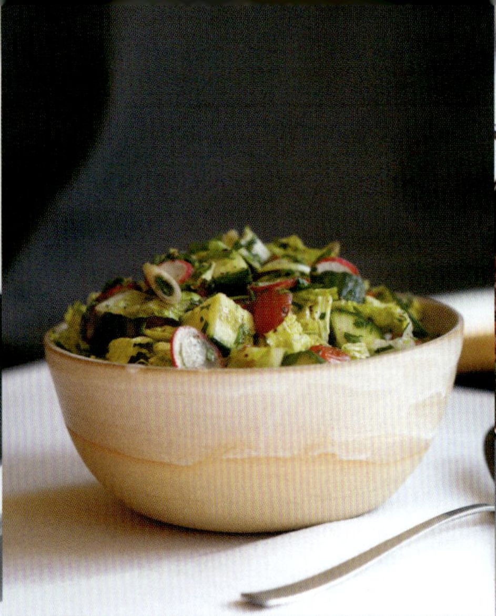
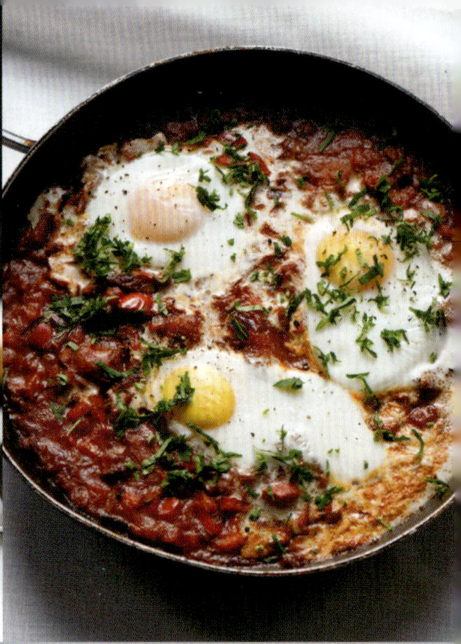
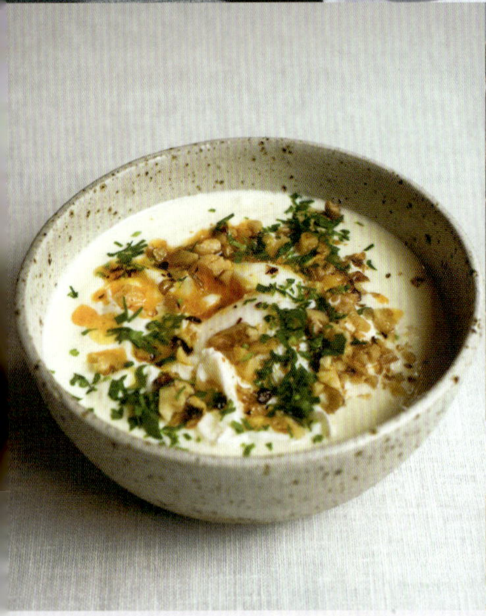
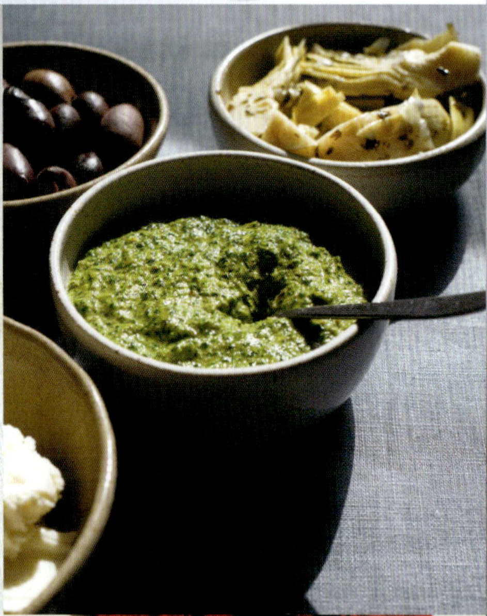
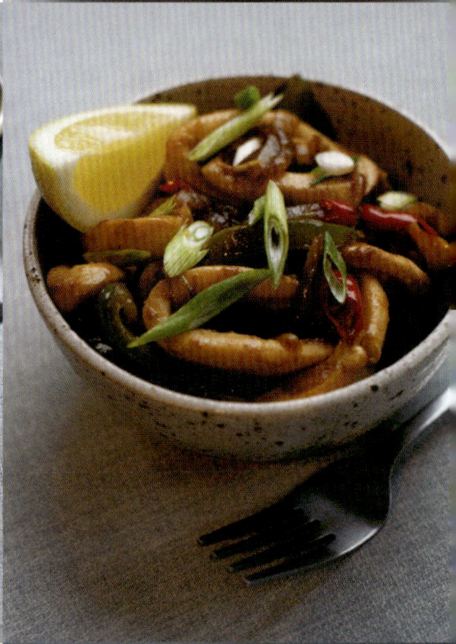
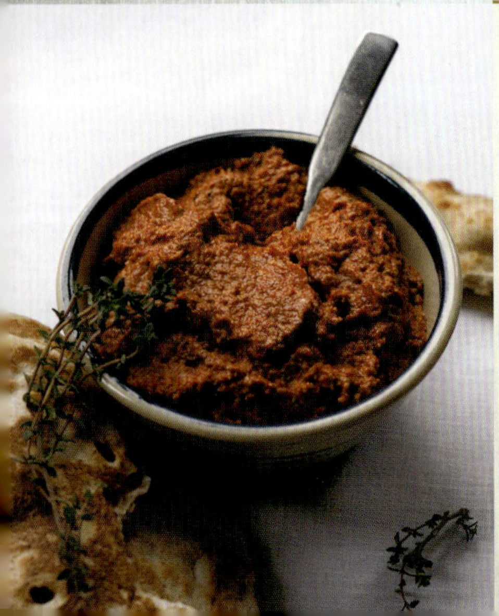
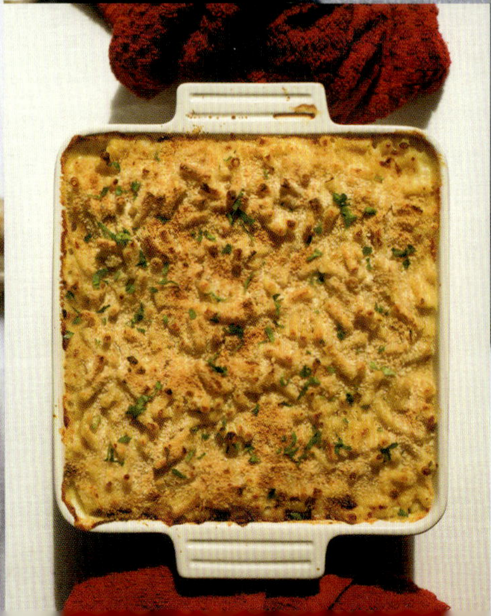
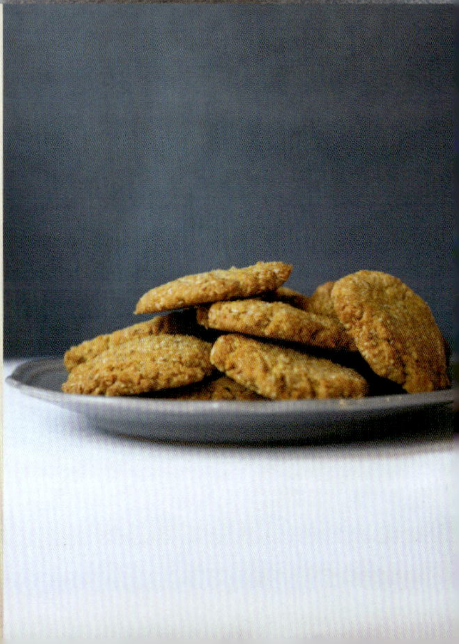

CONTENTS

Timeline	14
Meet the Artists	16
Handy Tools & Alternatives	26
Lebanon	28
Tunisia	34
Italy	38
Peru	44
Mexico	48
Thailand	54
Eritrea	60
Spain	64
Trinidad & Tobago	68
Mali	74
Sri Lanka	78
Argentina	84
Japan	88
Philippines	94
Turkey	98
Poland	104
Pakistan	108
New Zealand	114
Jamaica	118
Cuba	124
Stocks	128
Future Plans	133
Index	134

JANUARY 2020

We put out an open call for artists based in Greater Manchester, Cheshire and North Wales, the 3 regions where our organisation delivers cookery workshops and outreach work.

CALL FOR ARTISTS

FEBRUARY 2020

Our selection panel chose the 20 artists who feature in this recipe book! They have a wide range of styles and are all at different stages in their careers.

APRIL 2020

Our response to the Coronavirus outbreak included pledging 5 million free licenses to our Cooking & Nutrition Portal, which helped us to support people across the UK via our charity partners.

JULY 2020

Our Social Enterprise Internship programme ran remotely for the first time, which enabled us to work with a group of talented young people from across the country!

AUGUST 2020

We launched an accompanying podcast to the book called *Share your Secrets!* Episodes included interviews with the artists, Bounceback Food CIC team and people from the featured countries.

OCTOBER 2020

We were finally able to restart our face-to-face cookery workshops and learning programmes in line with social distancing guidelines.

We launched our 'Back the Book' crowdfunding campaign to raise the funds required to commission all of the artists involved and support the development of our community cookery school.

MARCH 2020

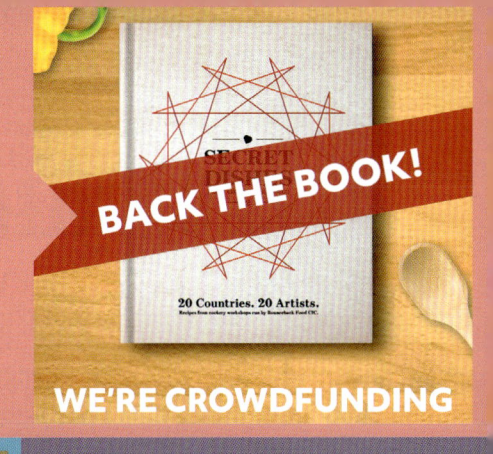

BACK THE BOOK!

WE'RE CROWDFUNDING

We completed the recipes, photography and additional graphic design work remotely while the country remained in lockdown.

MAY 2020

Artists submitted their original designs and profiles that feature in this book!

JUNE 2020

We started to deliver online cookery workshops and fundraising events, which allowed people across the UK to join our community cookery school.

SEPTEMBER 2020

We published *Secret Dishes From Around the World 2!*

NOVEMBER 2020

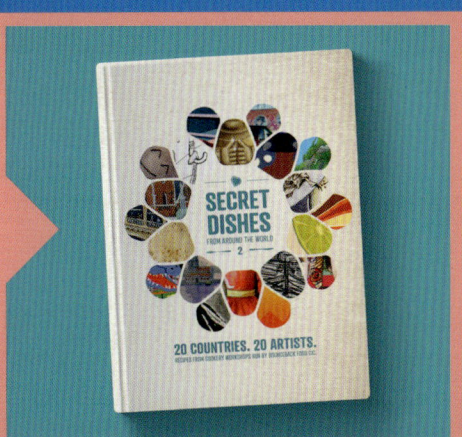

Head to page 133 to see what we've got planned...

THE FUTURE

JACK WHITELEGG

Jack studied Graphic Design at Stockport Art School and now runs Oll Korrect, a creative agency that supports a growing client base across Greater Manchester and the surrounding areas.

Country assigned Lebanon (see page 28)

About my work "For my piece I discovered that the capital city (Beirut) has been destroyed and rebuilt seven times which is why many refer to it as an urban phoenix. I took inspiration from tiles, mosaics and patterns found across Lebanon to create various shapes within the illustration."

Website www.okcreative.agency
Instagram @jackwhitelegg.design
Instagram @okcreative.agency

NATALIJA STOLAROVA

Natalija specialises in printmaking, illustration and stop motion animation. She has a particular interest in folklore and explores this through a variety of traditional and contemporary platforms.

Country assigned Tunisia (see page 34)

About my work "My illustration was inspired by Tunisian culture, traditions and art. The piece celebrates the rich variety of patterns in their textiles and ceramics, mesmerising traditional dance culture and vivid colour palettes. I combined these visual influences in my representation of Tunisia."

Website www.nstillustration.co.uk
Facebook www.facebook.com/nstillustration
Instagram @nstillustration

BERNICE TACKLEY

Bernice is a fine artist from Northwich, Cheshire. She works mainly with acrylics or watercolours on canvas and paper. Over the course of her career she has won several awards and was a winning finalist on the BBC2 programme 'Show me the Monet'. One of her paintings is in the private collection of HRH The Duke of Kent.

Country assigned Italy (see page 38)

About my work "My montage of Italy was inspired by the famous tourist attractions: the Rialto Bridge and gondolier in Venice, the Colosseum in Rome, the Leaning Tower of Pisa and the Italian Lakes. With the addition of the Roman temple and statue, Venetian masks and the ice-creams, this is Italy! Who can resist humming 'O Sole Mio' (Just One Cornetto)?"

Website	www.dianabernicetackley.com
Facebook	www.facebook.com/bernicetackley
Instagram	@bernicetackley

SAM TOMSON

Sam is a graphic designer and illustrator based in Manchester. Mainly self-taught, he discovered design after completing a Sociology degree. His work is rooted in and informed by music which has led to producing rave flyers and record artwork for a range of clients and labels.

Country assigned Peru (see page 44)

About my work "This piece pays homage to the rich pre-colonial history of Peru and depicts two deities. The red sun is Inti, the Sun God worshipped by the Incan culture. The Golden Tumis, meaning knife in Quechua (an indigenous language spoken in the Peruvian Andes), portrays Naylamp, the Lambayeque or Sicán God, from a culture preceding the Incans. Both are symbols of good luck!"

Instagram   @samuel.tomsky

MICHAEL WYLIE

Michael's artwork is focussed on hand-drawn typography and illustration. He aims to create art that starts a conversation and causes you to reminisce. He also runs Sketchbook Design, an organisation that produces stunning art prints and wall murals that transform any available space!

Country assigned Mexico (see page 48)

About my work "Mexican culture has strong ties to family and food. My research led me to a common quote which is used to support loved ones when they are going through tough times. 'Las penas con pan son menos' translates as 'All griefs are less with bread.' This phrase also encapsulates the ethos and work of Bounceback Food who support people through cooking and education."

Website www.sketchbookdesign.co.uk
Facebook www.facebook.com/sketchbookdesignuk
Instagram @sketchbookdesign_uk

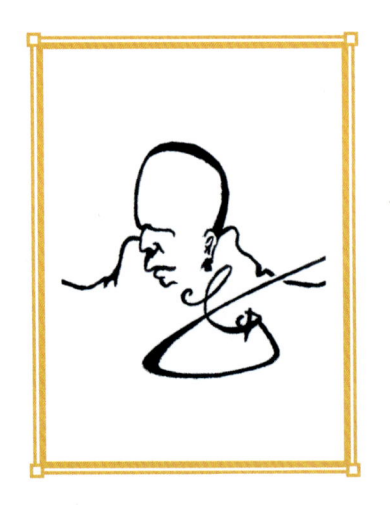

TOMMY BRADLEY

Tommy is a Manchester-based artist who grew up in Saddleworth, Oldham. His distinct style involves creating scenescapes with different gradients of Biro and is instantly recognisable. Tommy is keen to support the development of our community cookery school and admires our proactive approach to fighting food poverty.

Country assigned Thailand (see page 54)

About my work "Using the trusty Biro I wanted to depict a rather hectic and compact scenescape, one that would conjure up the visual bombardment of Thai city streets. As soon as you step out and bear witness, your senses are immediately in overdrive. The fragrance of sizzling, spiced street dishes, all freshly cooked in front of your eyes, is striking!"

Email tcb2@outlook.com

LYDIA FERNANDEZ-ARIAS

Lydia is a self-taught textile artist who loves experimenting with freehand embroidery! Her recent themes have been about women of the world and endangered British wildlife. In her free time, Lydia volunteers at two psychiatric hospitals in Manchester where she runs art workshops for patients. This has given her first-hand experience of the healing benefits of creativity.

Country assigned Eritrea (see page 60)

About my work "Coffee ceremonies are an integral part of daily life in Eritrea. Green coffee beans are roasted over hot coals, each person wafting the aromatic smoke over themselves. Once ground and brewed, the coffee is poured from a jebena into small cups on a low table. It is an important way for families and friends to relax together each day."

Facebook   www.facebook.com/artlydelights

VICTORIA REBEKAH

Victoria is a traditional artist based in Sandbach, Cheshire. Her work has been showcased in art trails and exhibitions around the North West and she has also competed in the Manchester Art Battle! She travels around Cheshire teaching art to home educated children and young adults with autism. Her current theme of work is portraiture using a variety of mixed media.

Country assigned Spain (see page 64)

About my work "I used a wide variety of media to create this piece including acrylic paints, watercolours, ink, drawing pens and coloured pencils. The flamenco dancer's dress is red and yellow to symbolise the Spanish flag. For the background, I decided to draw a building with arches, a very common feature in Spanish architecture."

Facebook   www.facebook.com/victoriasartspace
Instagram   @victoriasartstudio
Instagram   @victoriasartclasses

EMMA REYNOLDS

Emma is a children's book illustrator and author based in Manchester. She is passionate about storytelling, creating unique characters and is inspired by nature, animals, adventure and seeing the magic in the everyday! Emma also started the #KidLit4Climate illustrated campaign which brought together thousands of children's illustrators from over fifty countries in solidarity with the youth climate strikes.

Country assigned Trinidad & Tobago (see page 68)

About my work "I wanted to focus on fresh, mouth-watering ingredients and celebrate the bright colours and variety of shapes coming together like party confetti!"

Website www.emmareynoldsillustration.com
Instagram @emmaillustrate
Twitter @emmaillustrate

JAMES BLINKHORN

James is an established Cheshire-based artist who also runs Vermilion Art Gallery in Knutsford. His individual pieces and collections are owned by an array of private and corporate collectors throughout the UK, Europe and America. He is inspired by unconventional outdoor scenes melding different shapes, colours and textures together in unusual ways to form alternative perspectives.

Country assigned Mali (see page 74)

About my work "I took my inspiration from an imagined riverboat trip along the Niger, experiencing the people and towns along the way. Strolling around the ancient trading city of Djenné, you'd see its Moroccan-influenced architecture and the Grand Mosque, the world's largest mud building. There'd also be camel treks in the desert and tea drinking in Gao. What a trip - just need to do it now!"

Website www.vermiliongallery.co.uk
Instagram @vermilion.galleries
Twitter @vermilion_art

ALEXANDRA BOOCOCK

Alexandra is a digital illustrator who specialises in food. She was signed to Artworks London for the first two years of her career where she produced work for the Radio Times, Paperchase and Apples to Pears Ltd. Alex is now a full-time freelancer and runs Made By Rooted, a homeware gift company selling eco-friendly goods.

Country assigned Sri Lanka (see page 78)

About my work "My illustration is inspired by the food itself! The Sri Lankan cuisine has many delights for an illustrator who loves to draw food from all around the world. The unique shape and texture of Egg Appam is something that I thought deserves to stand out and be admired by everyone."

Website www.alexandraboocock.co.uk
Email alexandraboocock@yahoo.co.uk
Instagram @alexandraboocockillustration

PETER LANG

Peter is a Manchester-based freelance graphic designer who has supported the development of Bounceback Food CIC since day 1! During his career he has produced work for brands such as Kellogg's, O2 and Müller including infographics, branding, printed communications and digital marketing. Peter has also helped with the development of our sister social enterprise Bounceback Education, designing their learning centre shop front and online learning platform.

Country assigned Argentina (see page 84)

About my work "I really enjoyed researching this country and decided to create a montage to showcase the variety of Argentinian culture and geography. As a keen traveller, Argentina is now definitely on my bucket list!"

Website www.peterdoesdesign.co.uk

JESSICA OWEN

Jessica has painted professionally from her Manchester studio since 2003. She uses a wide array of paint mediums including sprays, enamel and oil to create her signature style of big brooding skies with a strong concentration on light and dark. Painting is a means of meditation for Jessica. She lets her work evolve naturally from one stage to the next.

Country assigned Japan (see page 88)

About my work "I wanted my painting to transport the reader. Mount Fuji, with its iconic profile, was an obvious choice for the start of this section. The purity of monotone painting, together with a loose and liberal use of watercolour, helped me to recreate this unmistakable national wonder."

Website www.northernscapes.co.uk
Instagram @jessica_owen_artist

RORY SPENCER

Rory is a part-time illustrator who also helps to run Snitch, a Manchester-based DIY publisher that aims to make the arts more accessible by breaking down barriers to entry into the creative industry. He wants to ensure that nobody is excluded from the food sector too, which is why he is keen to support our social enterprise.

Country assigned Philippines (see page 94)

About my work "Imagine that you were going to be stir-fried, seasoned and eaten - you'd try and fit in too!"

Website www.snitchpublishes.co.uk
Instagram @low_vagrancy
Instagram @snitchpublishes

JAMIE GRIFFITHS

Jamie is an emerging 3D modeller and animator based in Colwyn Bay, North Wales. He enjoys using CGI to convey artistic expression, technical testing and satirical whimsy which ensures his work has a distinct, surreal style.

Country assigned Turkey (see page 98)

About my work "My work was inspired by a view of the Maiden's Tower on the Champs de Mar in Istanbul. I wanted to capture the feel of an explorer coming to rest and digesting their experience of exploring Turkey. There are a few nods to Turkish culture for the knowledgeable. I really enjoyed bringing this piece to life!"

Facebook   www.facebook.com/jamie.f.griffiths

CHRISTIAN TURNER

Christian is a Cheshire-based artist who primarily works with oil paints. Some of his favourite subjects include marine life and birds and he enjoys incorporating geometry and maths into his work. Christian has exhibited in numerous open and private exhibitions. He has featured in local media including a brief editorial in Cheshire Life Magazine and an interview on RedShift Radio!

Country assigned Poland (see page 104)

About my work "It was fascinating to find out about the history and culture of Poland. It would be impossible to fit everything about their nation onto one canvas! I wanted to produce a piece that someone from Poland could recognise and identify as distinctly Polish."

Website   www.christianturnerart.com
Facebook   www.facebook.com/christianturnerart

HOLLY GORNE

Holly is a self-taught illustrator working mainly in acrylic, watercolour and digital illustration. She draws inspiration from a variety of sources, such as botanical sketches and religious iconography, though often incorporates her love of food and cooking into her work. She has produced artwork for multiple magazines and zines, as well as social media content for Time to Change.

Country assigned Pakistan (see page 108)

About my work "For this piece, I took inspiration from the patterns of ajraks, which are block-printed shawls traditional to the Sindh province in Pakistan. My aim was to incorporate the ingredients into the design of the fabric, representing the way that food is such an integral part of any culture."

Instagram   @hollygorne

EMILY GIBBS

Emily is based in Conwy, North Wales. She draws inspiration from both Japanese Anime and Manga then adds a modern twist of punk and rock! As well as her design for New Zealand, Emily produced a bespoke piece for our 'Back the Book' crowdfunding campaign which helped raise the funds required to publish this book.

Country assigned New Zealand (see page 114)

About my work "There is an ancient Maori legend that tells the story of a demigod that landed on a live stingray, transforming it into New Zealand! My piece depicts this scene and shows what the country might have looked like when the stingray was alive. The symbol in the sky means Koru and represents new life and growth."

Email   emilygibbs1111@gmail.com

AMBERLEY GARLAND

Amberley is a freelance illustrator based in central Manchester. She has a distinct abstract style that uses bright colours to create thought-provoking work. Her piece 'Humans and their Habitats' recently won the Aon Community Art Award 2018/19. Amberley also helped to design the interior of the first Bounceback Education learning centre in Salford!

Country assigned Jamaica (see page 118)

About my work "Through my research I have been transported to Jamaica in all its splendour! I cooked up some yummy dishes, read children's books and watched documentaries to discover the wealth of culture and beauty Jamaica holds. The vibrant colours, lifestyle, natural surroundings, music, crafts and fashion have all inspired me."

Website www.amberleygarland.com
Instagram @amberleygarland

OLLIE HIRST

Ollie is a conceptual illustrator who aims to ensure his work has true purpose by representing real world issues. His graphic, eye-catching style and diverse portfolio has seen his work published in The Big Issue, The Financial Times, The Washington Post and led to collaborations with Adobe, WeTransfer and Vodafone.

Country assigned Cuba (see page 124)

About my work "When I was assigned Cuba, I could already see the colours and hear the music before I'd even worked out what I was going to draw! Located in the northern Caribbean, Cuba has a rich history rooted in community and so it was important for me to capture that."

Website www.olliehirst.co.uk
Instagram @olliehirstillustration

HANDY TOOLS & ALTERNATIVES

Here's our timeless advice on a selection of kitchen utensils that can help improve your cooking!

Knives

One well suited, versatile knife, looked after, will serve you much better than a whole set of specialist blades. When choosing a knife consider how comfortable you are with its weight and size. We recommend a medium to large chef's knife as a good, all purpose home kitchen option. Small knives will struggle to chop more hardy vegetables and a larger, heavier knife can be a little cumbersome and tiring to hold if you are not used to them.

Pans

A couple of medium sized saucepans will see you through most dishes in this book. Every cuisine in the world makes use of pan frying and so it's worth finding one you can use over and over for different dishes. Use a tawa pan for the chapatis (see page 113) and an appa pan for the egg appam (see page 83) if you have them. If not, a conventional non-stick frying pan is a good alternative.

Spice Mixers

For the strongest flavours, grinding fresh spices with a pestle and mortar is usually best. One made out of stone will work as well as other more expensive (granite) options, they are relatively cheap too. Once bought they will last a lifetime and they can really help bring your dishes to life! If you don't have a pestle and mortar, you can mix together pre-ground herbs in a bowl with a teaspoon instead.

Blenders

While the price of some premium blenders can reach astronomical heights, simple hand blenders can be found for about £10 in most larger supermarkets or appliance retailers. These handy little tools are great for liquifying soups, curries and purées. A half decent one will also make quick work of awkward tasks like chopping nuts, though this can also be achieved by careful chopping with a knife. Blenders with a chamber fitting are also excellent for making pesto.

Although blenders are perhaps not quite a kitchen essential, they are certainly worth considering especially if you find the labour of excessive chopping difficult or if you are cooking for someone who struggles with solid foods.

Spatula, Tongs and Spoons

When buying these kitchen essentials, you'll need to consider how frequently you'll use them and remember what they're best for! Spatulas are essential for pancake style flipping and are useful for scraping stuck food from the bottom of a pan. Tongs are good for flipping vegetables in the pan but not as good for trying sauces. Spoons are great for testing and stirring sauces but can make it difficult to flip food such as onion slices which can stick flat to the pan.

You'll also need to consider the material that utensils are made from. Metal and plastic tools are more hygienic and easier to clean. However, if a plastic tool is not heat resistant it can melt on a hot surface. Metal tools can damage the bottom of a pan when used incorrectly.

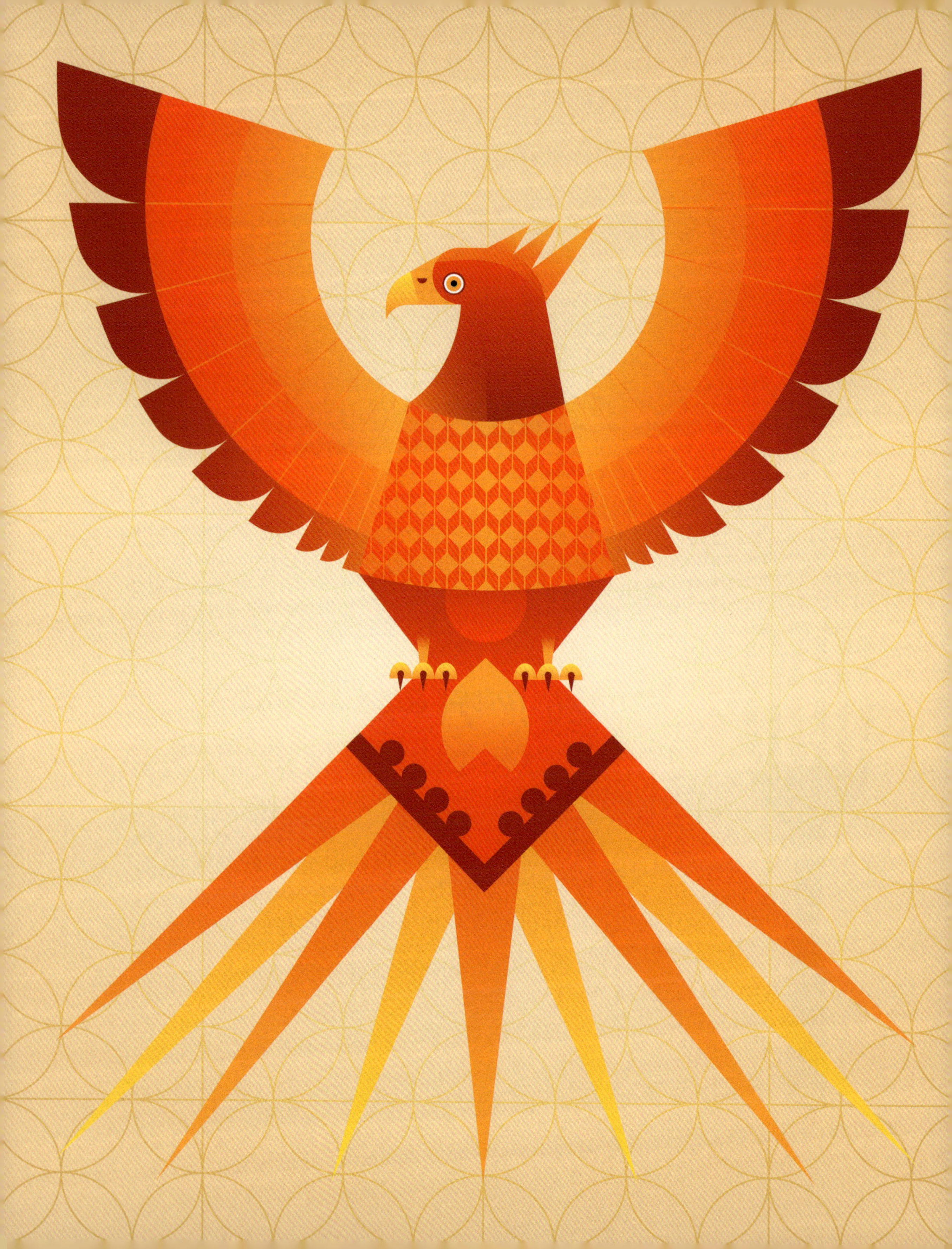

LEBANON

Art by Jack Whitelegg

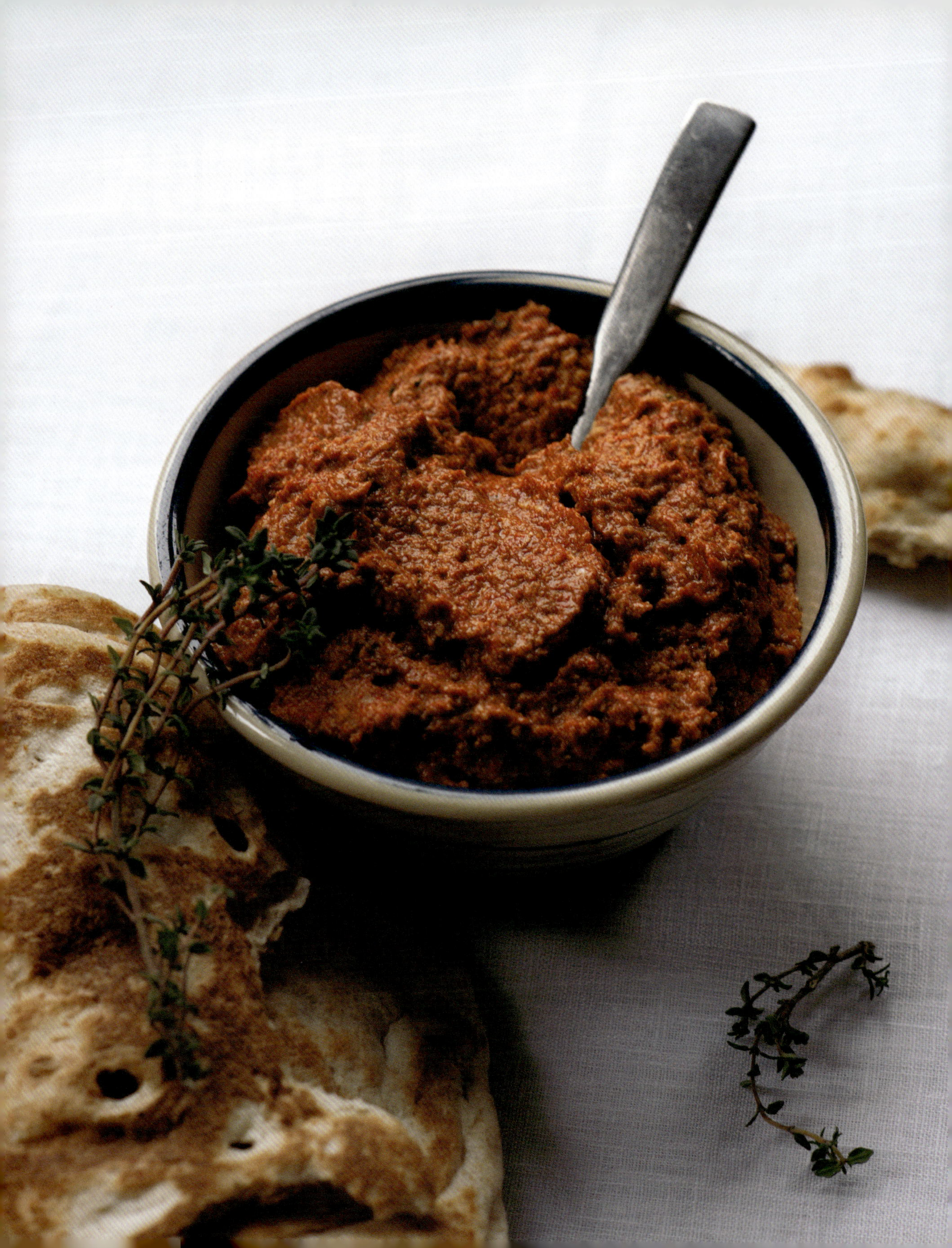

MUHAMMARA

Serves 4 | 60 mins | Vegetarian

A delicious dip to add to your Middle Eastern meals, muhammara is made up primarily of charred peppers and walnuts.

INGREDIENTS

6 red peppers
90g walnuts, diced
60g dried breadcrumbs
Juice of half a lemon
1 tbsp pomegranate molasses
2 tsps ground cumin
3 garlic cloves, roughly chopped
2-3 tbsps olive oil
Salt to taste
Handful of thyme leaves (optional)

METHOD

1. Pre-heat the oven to 200°C. Place the peppers on an oiled oven tray and put in the oven. Cook until blacked all over, turning the peppers once in a while to ensure an even cook.

2. In a pan over a low-medium heat toast the nuts for approx. 1 minute then place to one side.

3. Once the peppers are charred all over remove from the oven tray and place in a large bowl. Cover the lid of the bowl with cling film until the peppers are cool enough to handle.

4. Once the peppers have cooled sufficiently, remove the cling film. Now peel all the skin from the peppers and discard. Also remove seeds, stalk and core at the same time.

5. Now add the peppers, walnuts and all the other ingredients into a blender, mixing together into an even consistency. Adjust the ingredients for a texture and flavour which you prefer.

Chef's tips

Fresh thyme leaves also help to enhance the flavour.
VEGAN SWITCH Just make sure your breadcrumbs are vegan!

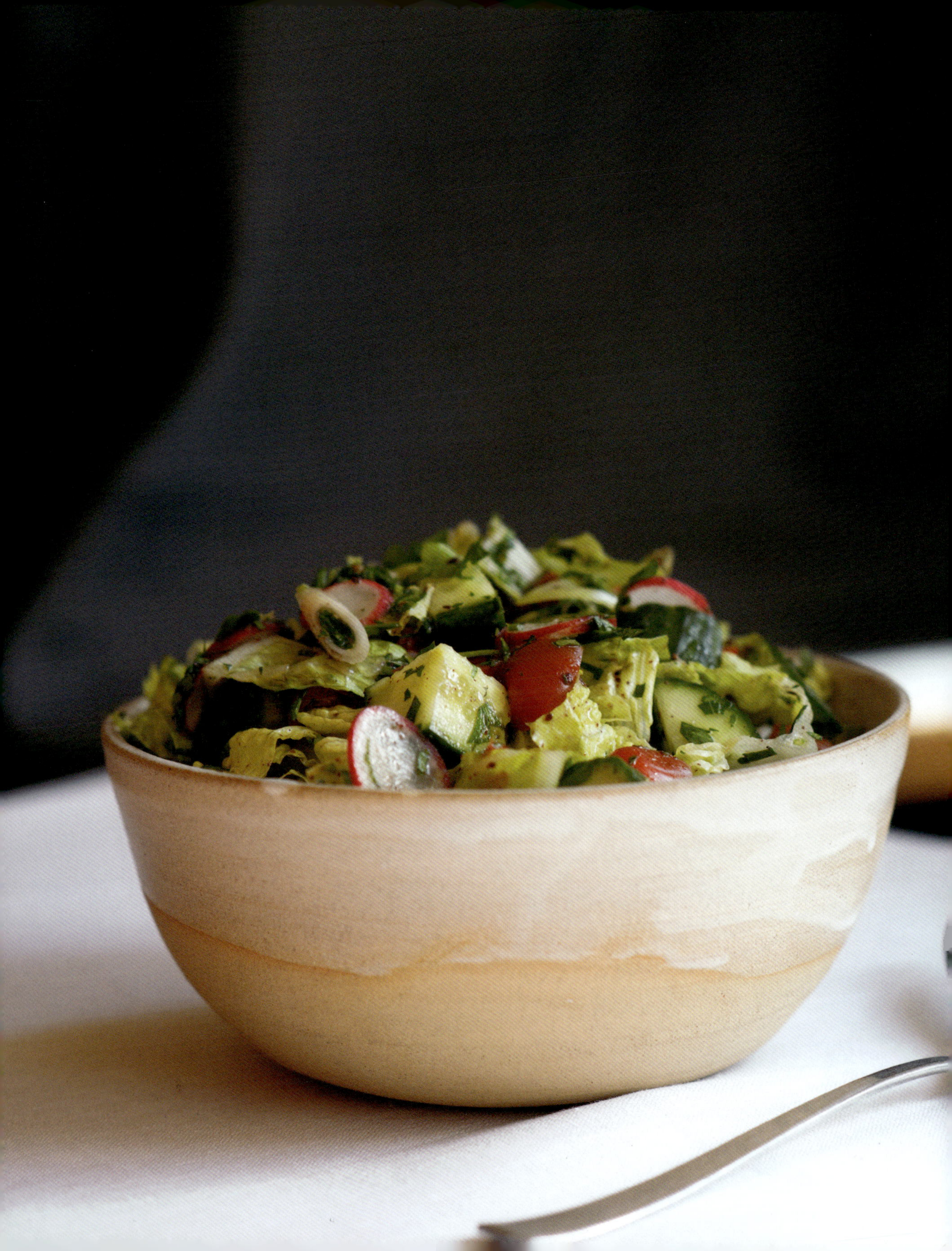

FATTOUSH

Serves 6 | **25 mins** | **Vegan**

The perfect, healthy accompaniment to many Middle Eastern meals.

INGREDIENTS

- 120g fresh parsley, finely chopped
- 1 cucumber, chopped
- 120g fresh tomatoes, chopped
- 90g radish, thinly sliced
- 50g spring onion, sliced
- 90g lettuce, roughly chopped
- 2 pitta breads, roughly chopped
- 5 tbsps olive oil
- Juice of 1 lemon
- Salt to taste
- Handful of mint leaves, finely chopped (optional)
- Sumac (optional)

METHOD

1. In a mixing bowl, drizzle olive oil and a pinch of salt over the pieces of bread so that most of their surface area is covered.
2. Place a pan over a medium heat. Add the bread and fry for 3 minutes or until browning appears. Flip and repeat.
3. Combine the bread with all the other ingredients in a large bowl. Mix thoroughly then serve.

Chef's tips: Top this dish with extra olive oil, chopped mint leaves or a dusting of sumac.

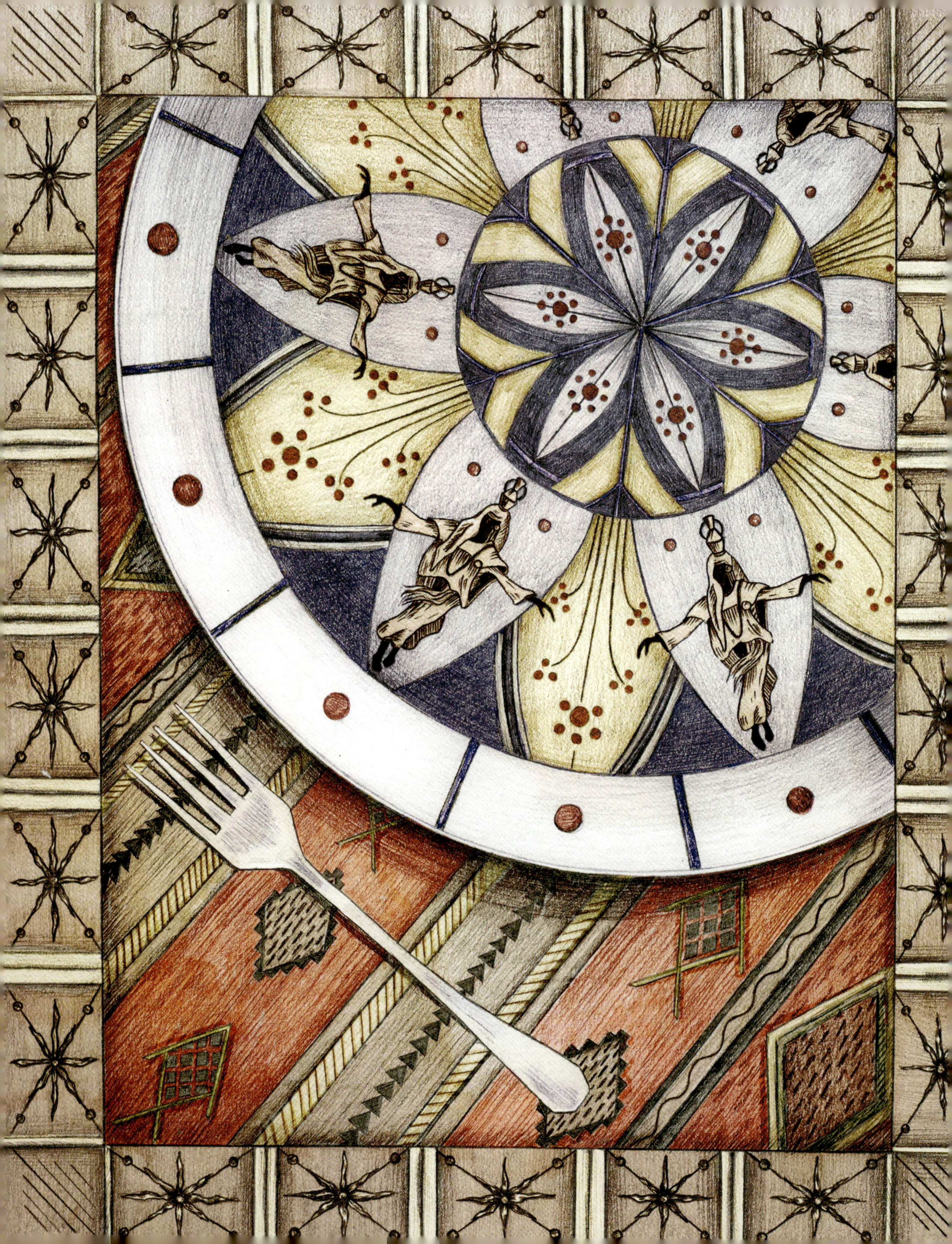

TUNISIA

Art by Natalija Stolarova

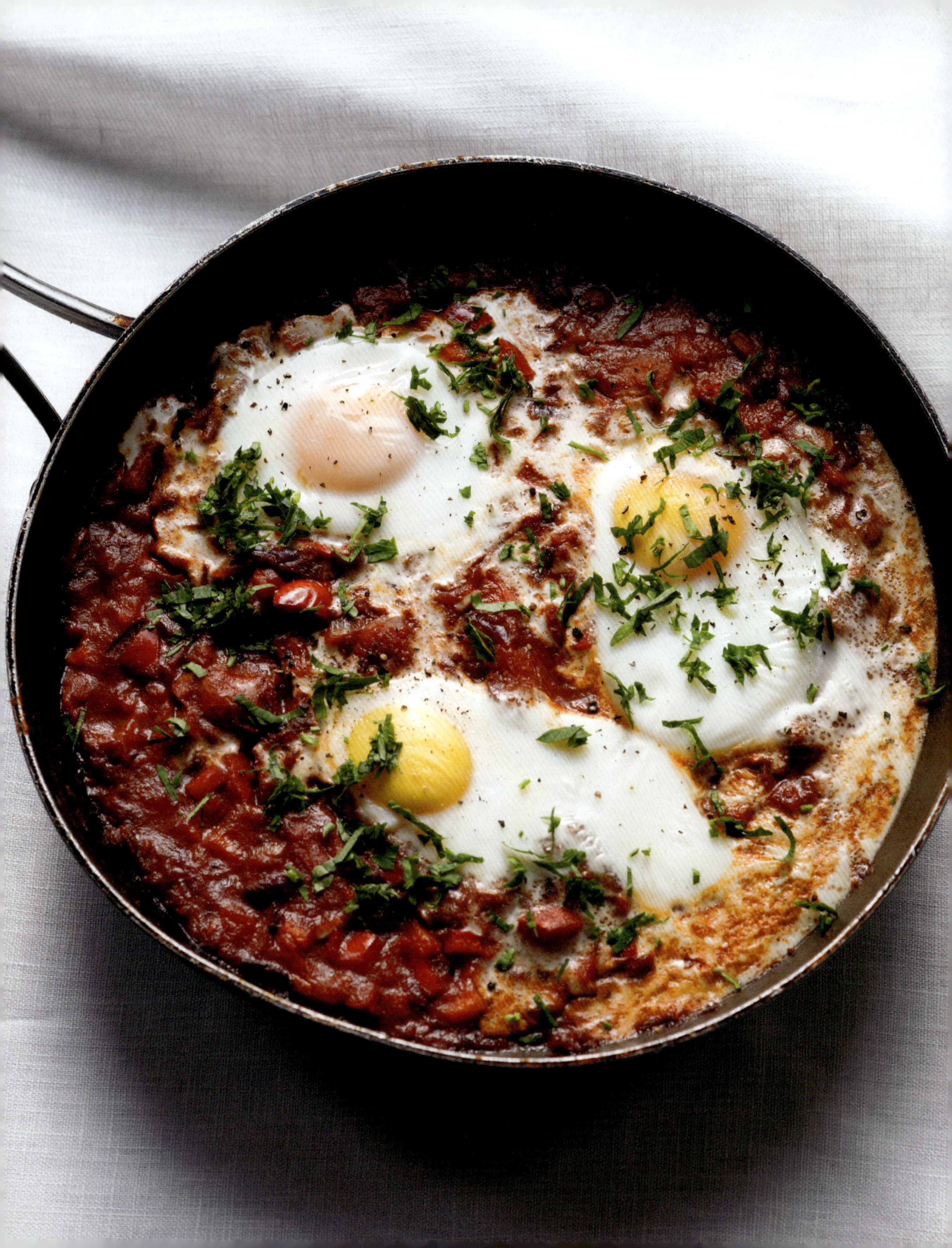

SHAKSHOUKA

Serves 3-4 | 30 mins | Vegetarian

A delicious feast of eggs, poached in a cumin-infused tomato sauce.

INGREDIENTS

1 tbsp olive oil
½ red onion, diced
1 garlic clove, crushed
1 red pepper, finely chopped
400g tin of chopped tomatoes
1 tbsp tomato purée
1 tsp smoked paprika
½ tsp mild chilli powder
1 tsp ground cumin
1 egg per person
Handful of fresh parsley, finely chopped
Salt and pepper

METHOD

1. Add the olive oil to a large pan over a medium heat. Add the onion and sauté for 5 minutes or until soft.
2. Add the garlic and chopped pepper. Cook for a few more minutes until they are soft too.
3. Stir in the tomatoes, tomato purée and spices. Simmer for a further 5 minutes until the sauce starts to reduce. Season with salt and pepper.
4. Lower the heat then crack the eggs directly over the tomato sauce. Place a lid on the pan and cook for a further 5 minutes or until the egg whites are firm and the yolks still runny. Garnish with chopped parsley and serve.

Chef's tips

Serve on bread or toast to turn this dish into a hearty brunch.
You can also cook the eggs by placing the pan under a grill.
VEGAN SWITCH Replace the eggs with pan-fried tofu or roasted chickpeas.

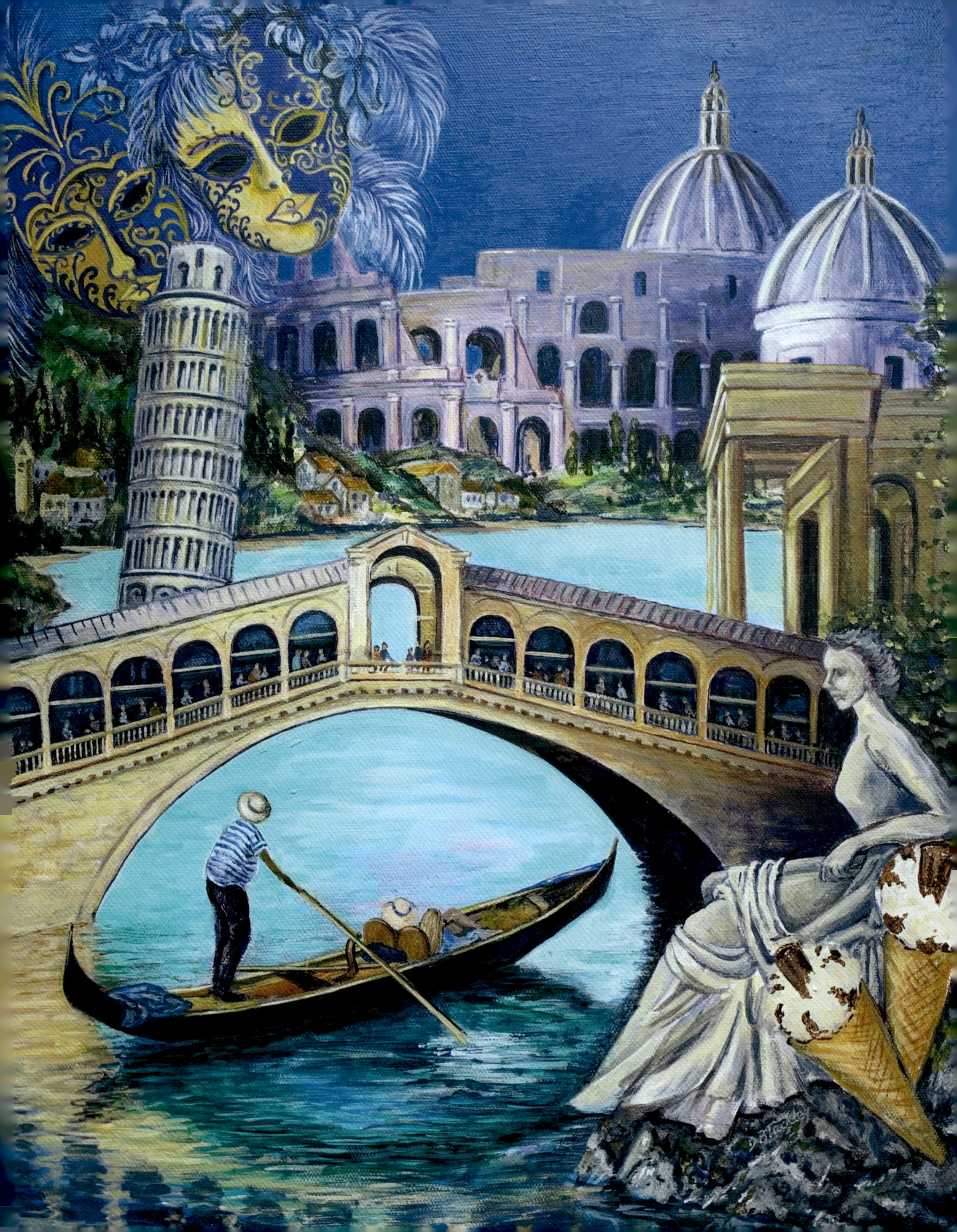

ITALY

Art by Bernice Tackley

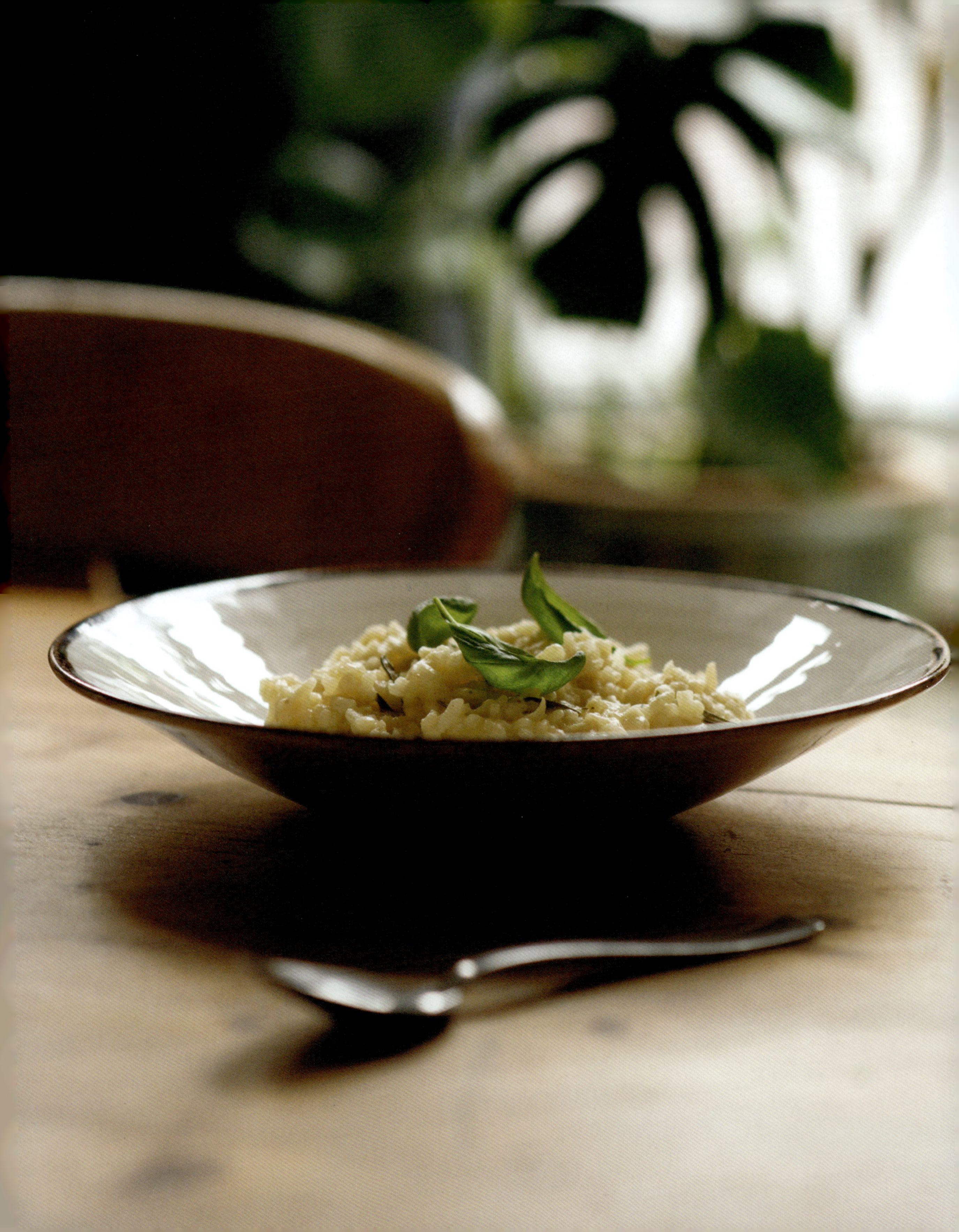

RISOTTO

Serves 4-6

45 mins

This Italian classic is a perfect alternative to pasta.

INGREDIENTS

500g arborio rice
1 brown onion, diced
2 garlic cloves, crushed
1½ litres vegetable stock
200g parmesan, grated
3 stalks of rosemary
2 tbsps olive oil
Salt to taste
Pesto (optional)

METHOD

1. Dry fry the the rice on a low heat for 1 minute, do not allow to toast. Then place into a large bowl and leave to one side.
2. Add the olive oil to a large pan over a medium heat. Add the onions and a pinch of salt to help soften them.
3. Add the garlic and fry with the onions until both are soft.
4. Re-add the rice and cover with two-thirds of the stock. Raise heat to a simmer.
5. Add the rosemary. Stir regularly as the rice cooks, incrementally adding the remaining stock to ensure that the dish stays hydrated enough to cook the rice and not stick to the pan.
6. When the rice is almost cooked it will release starch into the mix and this will begin to bind the dish into a porridge-like consistency. Cook for a further 2-3 minutes to remove any excess liquid.
7. Remove the rosemary stalks.
8. Slowly add the parmesan and mix through until melted.

Chef's tips

Remember to test your rice before serving to ensure that there is no chalky, uncooked texture remaining. Add pesto (see page 43) for a final flourish!
VEGAN SWITCH Use vegan parmesan and vegan-friendly vegetable stock.

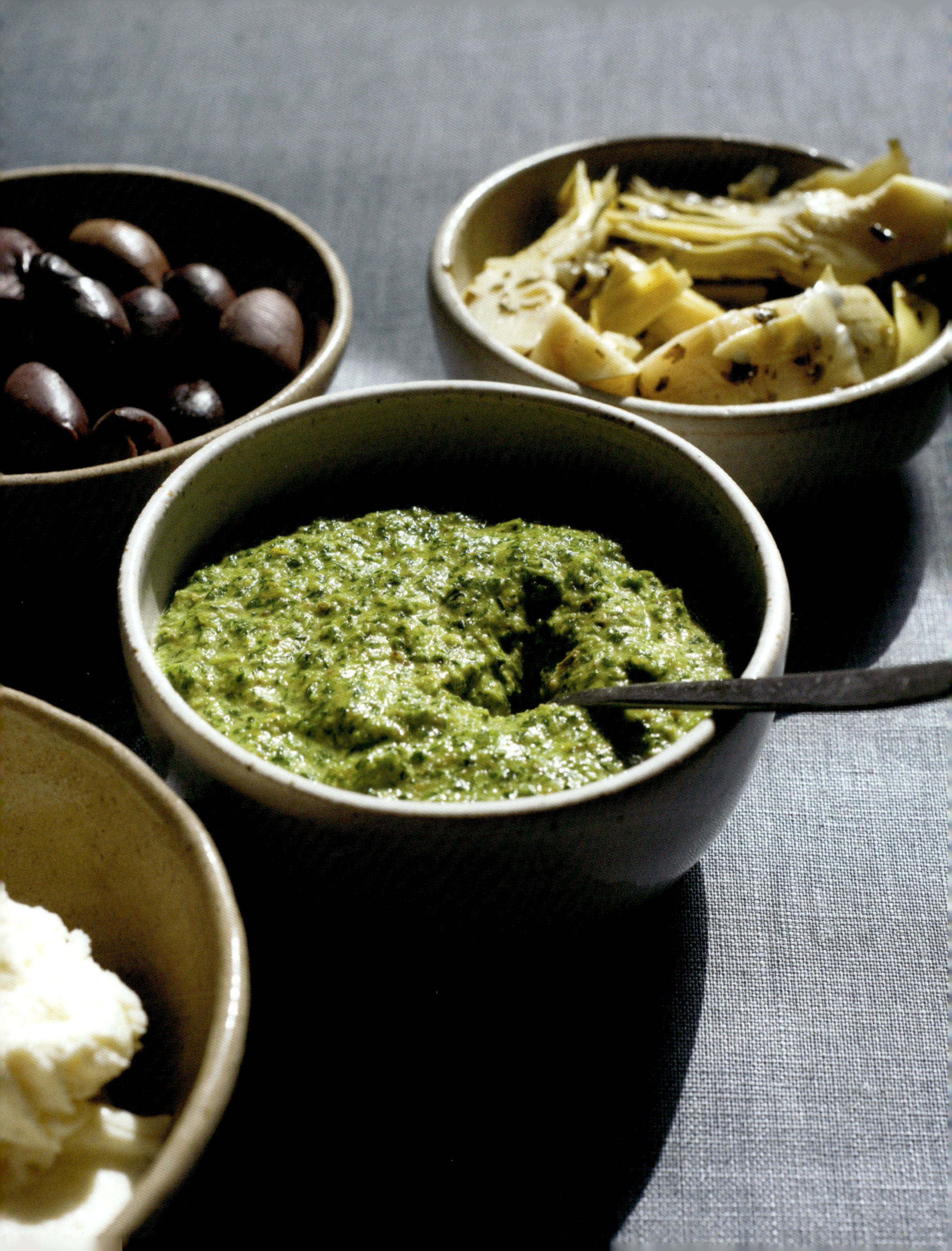

PESTO

Serves 4-6 | **20 mins** | **Vegan**

This Italian classic is easy to make and delicious!

INGREDIENTS

30g basil
20g spinach
50g pine nuts
1 garlic clove
3 tbsps capers
3 tbsps olive oil
Juice and zest of 1 lemon
Salt and pepper to taste

METHOD

1. Dry fry half of the pine nuts for 1 minute.
2. Remove them from the pan then add to a blender together with all the other ingredients.
3. Blend to a smooth consistency and serve with the remaining pine nuts as an optional garnish.

Chef's tips

A classic pesto would include parmesan but this version is vegetarian and vegan-friendly. Add extra crushed garlic if you want more of a kick!

Incan Ceremonial Tumis Knife

PERU

Art by Sam Tomson

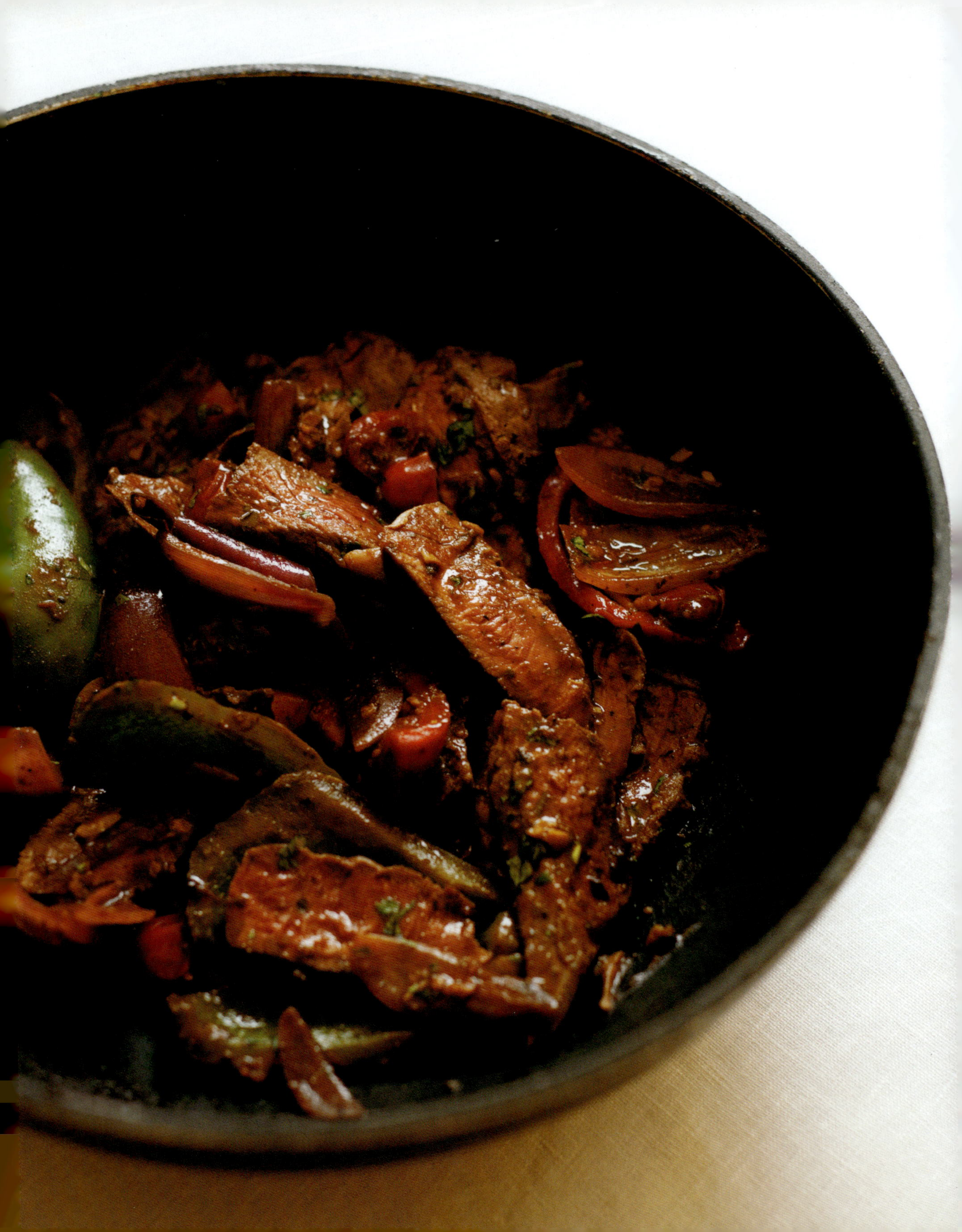

LOMO SALTADO

Serves 3-4 | 45 mins +120 mins marinating

A Peruvian street food sensation.

INGREDIENTS

FOR THE MARINADE
4 tbsps light soy sauce
1½ tsps ground cumin
2 tsps dried oregano
Salt and pepper to taste

FOR THE STIR FRY
400g beef steak
2 garlic cloves, crushed
1 tbsp vegetable oil
1 tsp smoked paprika
1 bell pepper, core removed and cut into large segments
1 red onion, chopped into large segments
150g tomatoes, chopped
1 tbsp chilli sauce
Handful of fresh coriander, finely chopped (optional)

METHOD

1. Add all the marinade ingredients into a mixing bowl including the beef and stir thoroughly. Cover with cling film then leave in the fridge to marinate for ideally 2 hours.

2. Remove mixing bowl from the fridge and allow the beef to stand for 20 minutes. Place a large pan or wok over a high heat and add the vegetable oil. Once hot, begin to cook the onions and pepper until both have begun to soften and browning has begun to appear on the peppers.

3. Add half the tomatoes, smoked paprika and chilli sauce. Cook for 5 minutes.

4. Remove the beef from the marinade and place to one side. Pour what remains of the marinade into the pan along with the garlic and remaining half of the tomatoes. Cook on a medium heat for 2 minutes then remove from the heat.

5. Add the vegetable oil to a second pan over a high heat and fry the beef to your liking. Once done, remove the beef to a chopping board and rest for 10 minutes before cutting into strips.

6. Add the strips of beef to your stir fry, bring up to temperature then serve.

chef's tips

Aji amarillo paste is used traditionally to give the heat to this dish but using a chilli sauce made from scotch bonnets will have a similar effect. Serve with rice or chips. Freshly chopped coriander also works well as an optional garnish.
VEGAN SWITCH Replace the beef with diced aubergine.

LAS PENAS CON PAN SON MENOS

MEXICO

Art by Michael Wylie

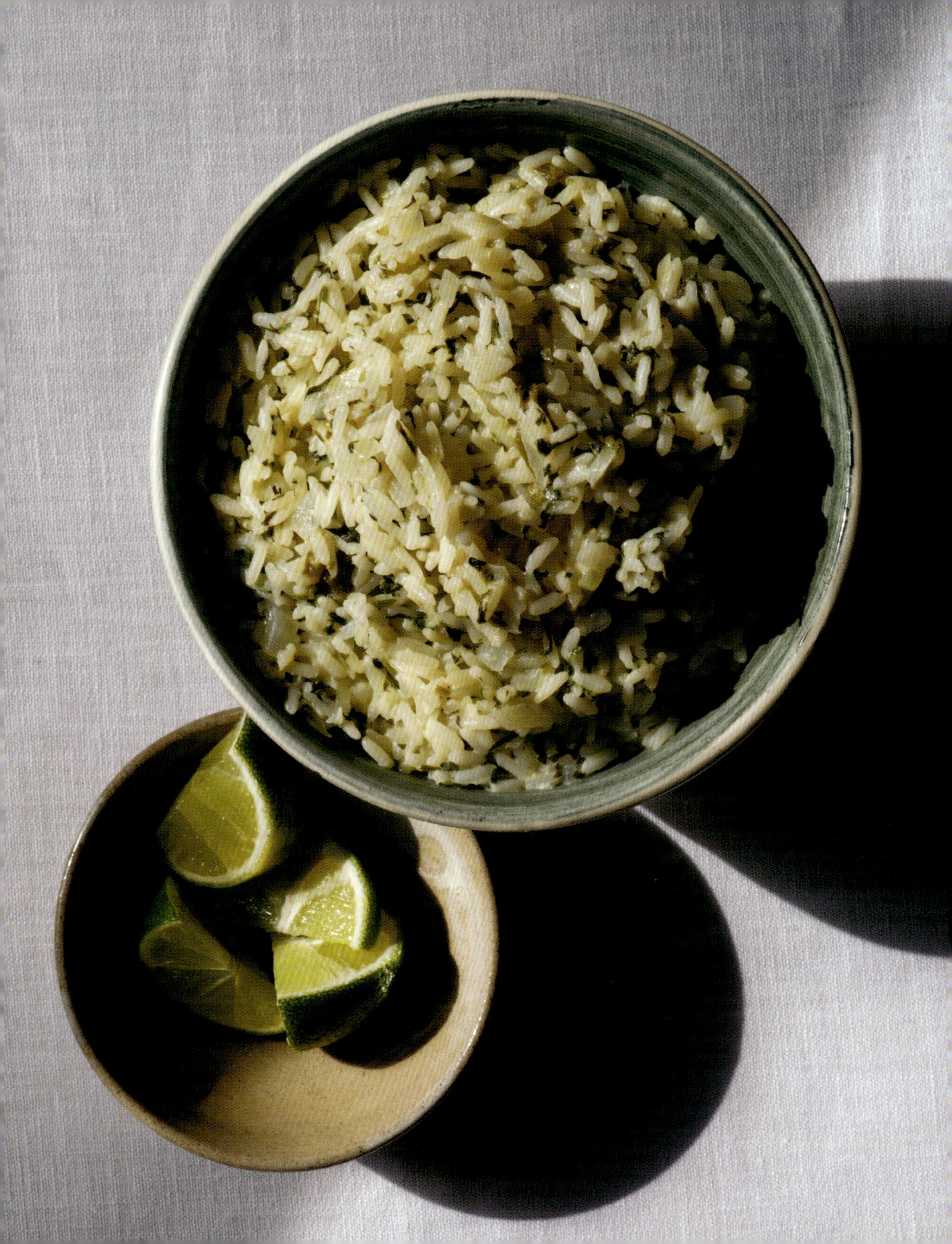

ARROZ VERDE

Serves 3-4 | 50 mins

Take cooking rice to the next level and try something new!

INGREDIENTS

25g jalapeños, roughly chopped
300ml milk
300ml chicken stock
300g long grain rice
1 brown onion, diced
3 garlic cloves, crushed
1 lime, quartered
Handful of spinach, finely chopped
Handful of fresh coriander, finely chopped
2 tbsps olive oil

METHOD

1. Combine the coriander, spinach and milk in a mixing bowl and leave to one side.
2. Add the olive oil to a large pan over a medium heat. Fry the rice for approx. 1 minute or until a light browning appears.
3. Add the onion, garlic and jalapeños and fry for a further minute.
4. Lower the heat, then add the milk mix and stock. Stir thoroughly and aim for an even consistency.
5. Bring the mixture to the boil. Once there, put the lid on the pan and reduce to a low heat.
6. Cook for 20 minutes or until the rice has cooked, stirring frequently towards the end. Loosen with more stock if required.

Chef's tips

Add extra jalapeños if you want more heat!
VEGAN SWITCH Use almond or oat milk and vegan-friendly vegetable stock for a delicious plant-based alternative.

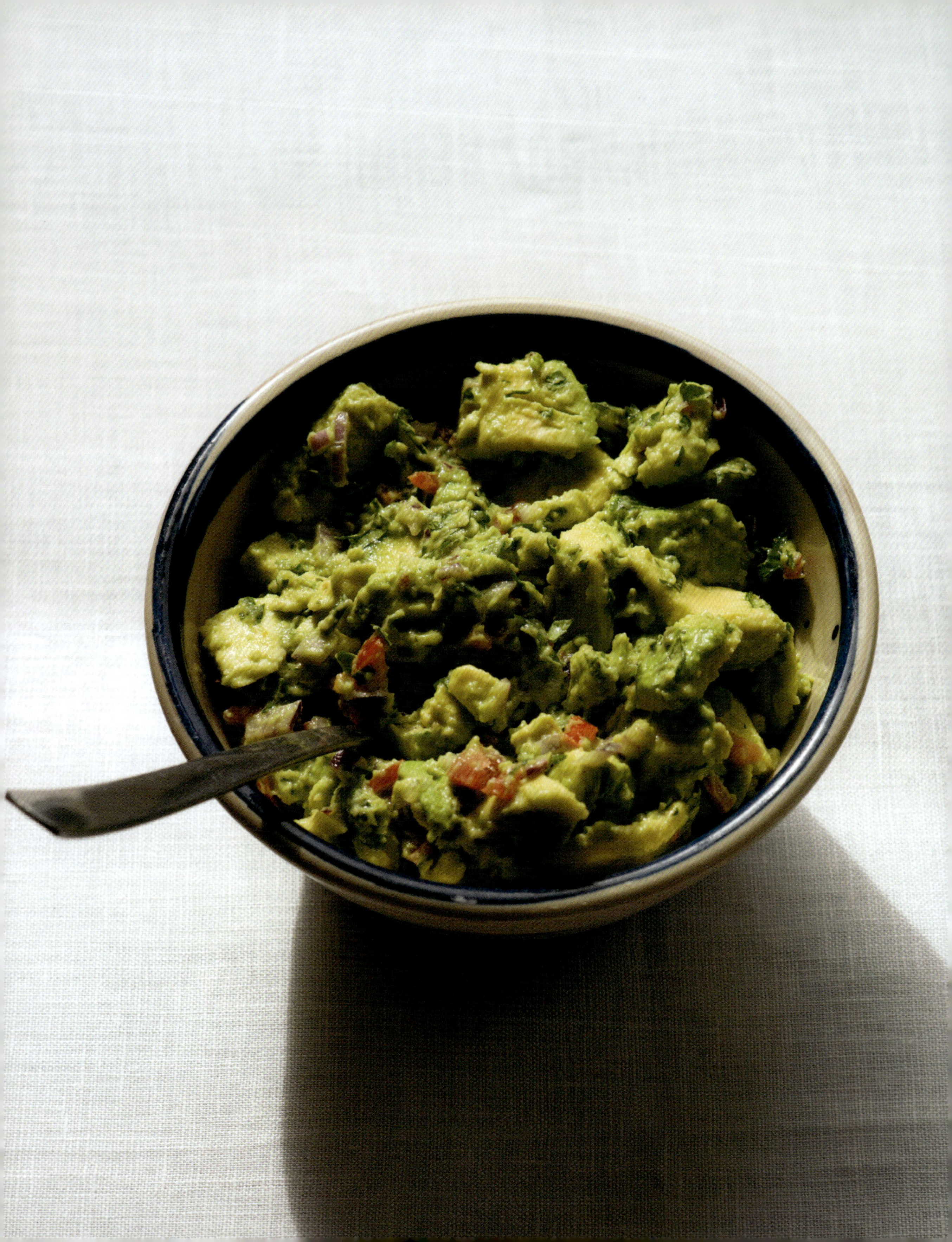

GUACAMOLE

Serves 4 | **20 mins** | **Vegan**

A magnificent, moreish side dish.

INGREDIENTS

- 2 large avocados, finely chopped
- ½ red onion, minced
- 1 medium tomato, finely chopped
- Handful of fresh coriander, finely chopped
- Juice of 2 limes
- 1 tsp chilli flakes
- Salt to taste

METHOD

1. Mix all ingredients in a large bowl.
2. Taste and adjust seasoning to your preference!

Chef's tips

Adjust the ingredient quantities to create your perfect flavour combination! Serve with tortilla chips or crudités.

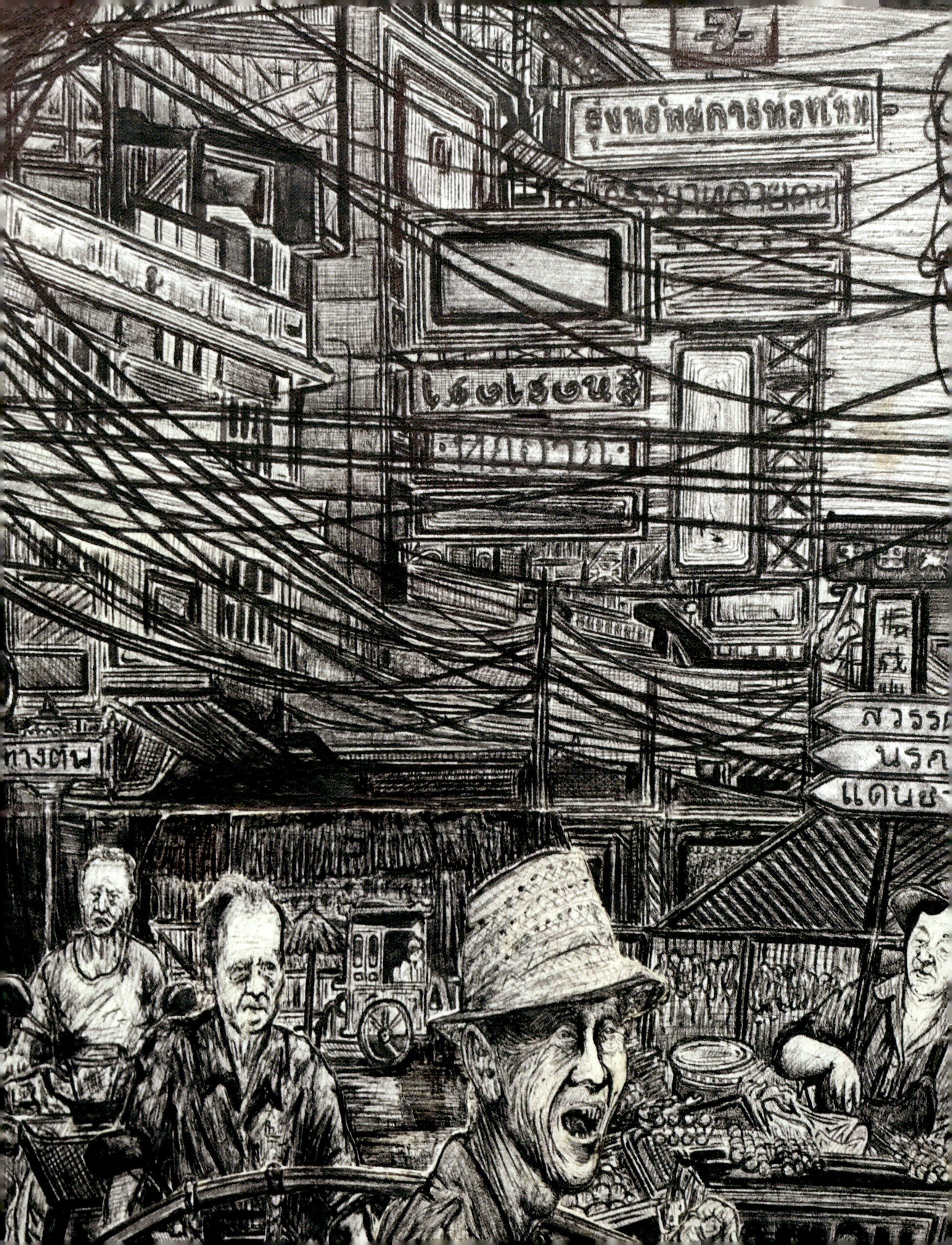

THAILAND

Art by Tommy Bradley

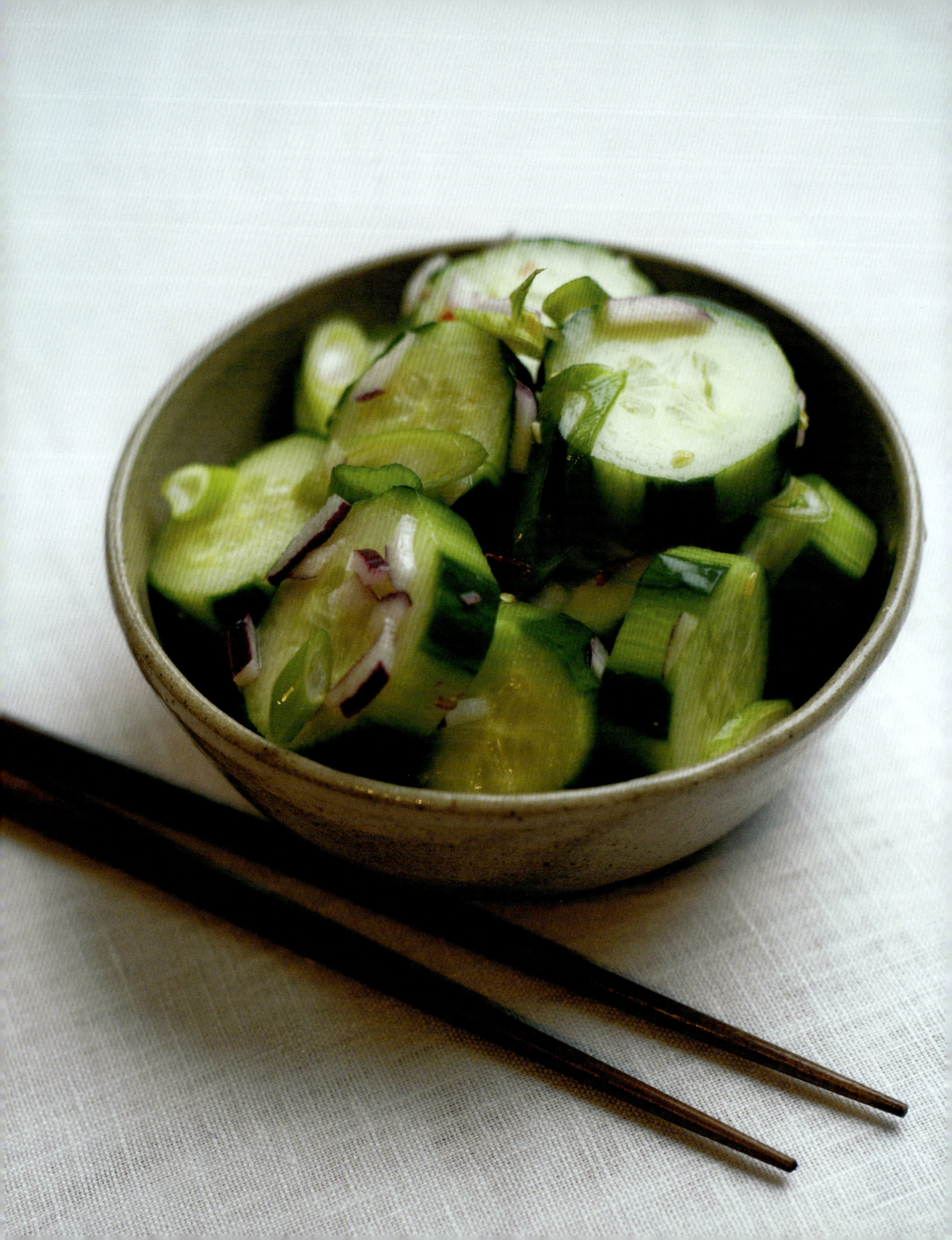

AJAT SALAD

Serves 4 | 180 mins | Vegan

A sharp and sweet side dish that serves perfectly with curries and stir-fries.

INGREDIENTS

FOR THE DRESSING
200ml rice vinegar
200ml water
200g sugar
3 tbsps salt

FOR THE SALAD
3 cucumbers, cut into slices
1 red onion, diced
3 red chillies, deseeded and finely chopped
100g spring onion, finely sliced

METHOD

1. Start by making the dressing 3 hours in advance of when you would like to eat. Combine the vinegar, water, sugar and salt in a pan then bring to the boil.
2. Simmer for 25 minutes or until the mixture has reduced to the consistency of a runny syrup.
3. Remove the pan from the heat then pour the syrup into a container. Wait until it has cooled to room temperature before transferring to the fridge.
4. Once the dressing is cold, prepare the ingriedients for the salad in a serving bowl.
5. Add the dressing to the salad and mix.
6. Leave to pickle in the fridge for 10 minutes then serve.

Chef's tips

Remember to taste and adjust your dressing as it reduces. Little adjustments here can make a big difference to the finished dish.
If you can't source rice vinegar, white wine vinegar can be used instead.

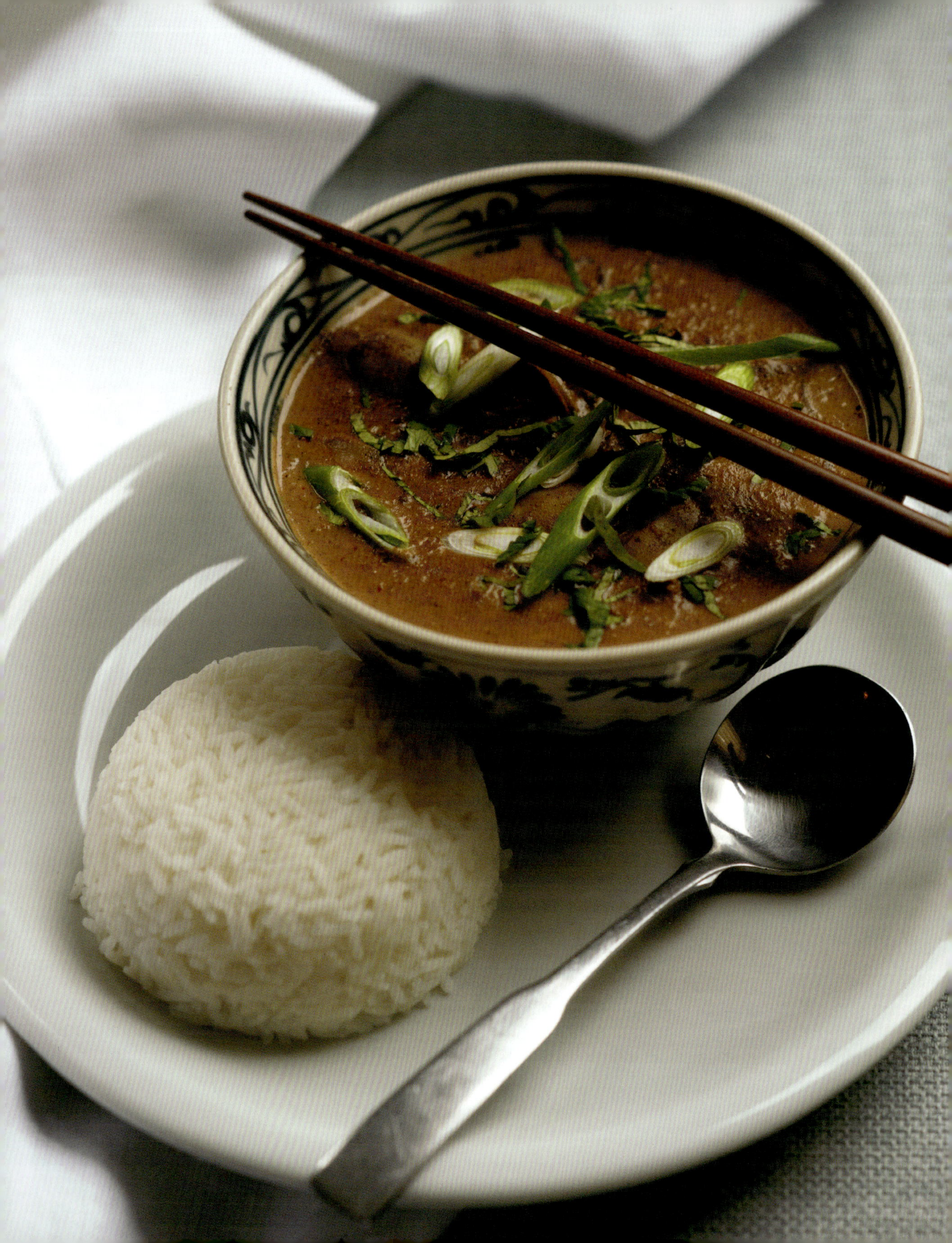

MASSAMAN CURRY

Serves 6

75 mins

This aromatic curry has a distinctive taste and is widely regarded as one of the world's favourite dishes.

INGREDIENTS

200g unsalted peanuts
70g ginger, peeled and roughly chopped
4 garlic cloves, roughly chopped
2 lemongrass stalks, thinly sliced
3 dried chillies
500g white potatoes, cubed and parboiled
20g palm sugar
8 tbsps tamarind sauce
800ml of coconut milk
1 brown onion, sliced
1 red onion, diced
2 tbsps fish sauce
1 tbsp fennel seeds
1½ tbsps coriander seeds
1½ tbsps cloves
6 cardamom pods, burst and shells discarded
1 tsp black peppercorns
2 tbsps ground cinnamon
Salt to taste
Handful of fresh coriander, finely chopped (optional)
1 lime (optional)
Rice (optional)
1 spring onion (optional)

METHOD

1. Pre-heat the oven to 180°C. Roast the peanuts on a baking tray until they are brown then leave them to one side to cool.

2. Dry fry the fennel seeds, coriander seeds, cloves, dried chillies and black peppercorns over a medium heat for 1 minute. Remove from the heat and transfer the ingredients to a pestle and mortar with the seeds from the burst cardamom pods. Crush to a powder then add the cinnamon and leave to one side.

3. Add the red onion, ginger, lemongrass and garlic to a frying pan. Carefully dry fry until a light browning occurs, adding the garlic last to ensure it doesn't burn. Once complete, add all the ingredients prepared so far to a blender and mix into a paste.

4. Add 3 tablespoons of coconut milk to a large pan over a medium heat. Once bubbling, mix in the spice paste and cook for 2 minutes. Add more coconut milk and reduce the heat if necessary.

5. Add the potatoes and coat evenly with the spice mix. Cook for a further 5 minutes, continuing to add coconut milk gradually if required to avoid sticking.

6. Pour in the remaining coconut milk and mix thoroughly. Add the brown onion, tamarind sauce, peanuts, fish sauce and enough water to sufficiently loosen the curry. Bring to a very gentle simmer.

7. Add the palm sugar and mix until dissolved. Place a lid on the pan and leave on a low simmer until the potatoes are cooked through. Cook on a low heat until the sauce is golden brown. Stir regularly and loosen with a dash of water if required.

Chef's tips

This dish is traditionally made with beef but our version uses extra potato instead. Use granulated sugar rather than palm sugar if you're struggling to source these ingredients. Serve with rice, lime wedges and a sprinkling of fresh coriander or spring onion.
VEGAN SWITCH Simply omit the fish sauce!

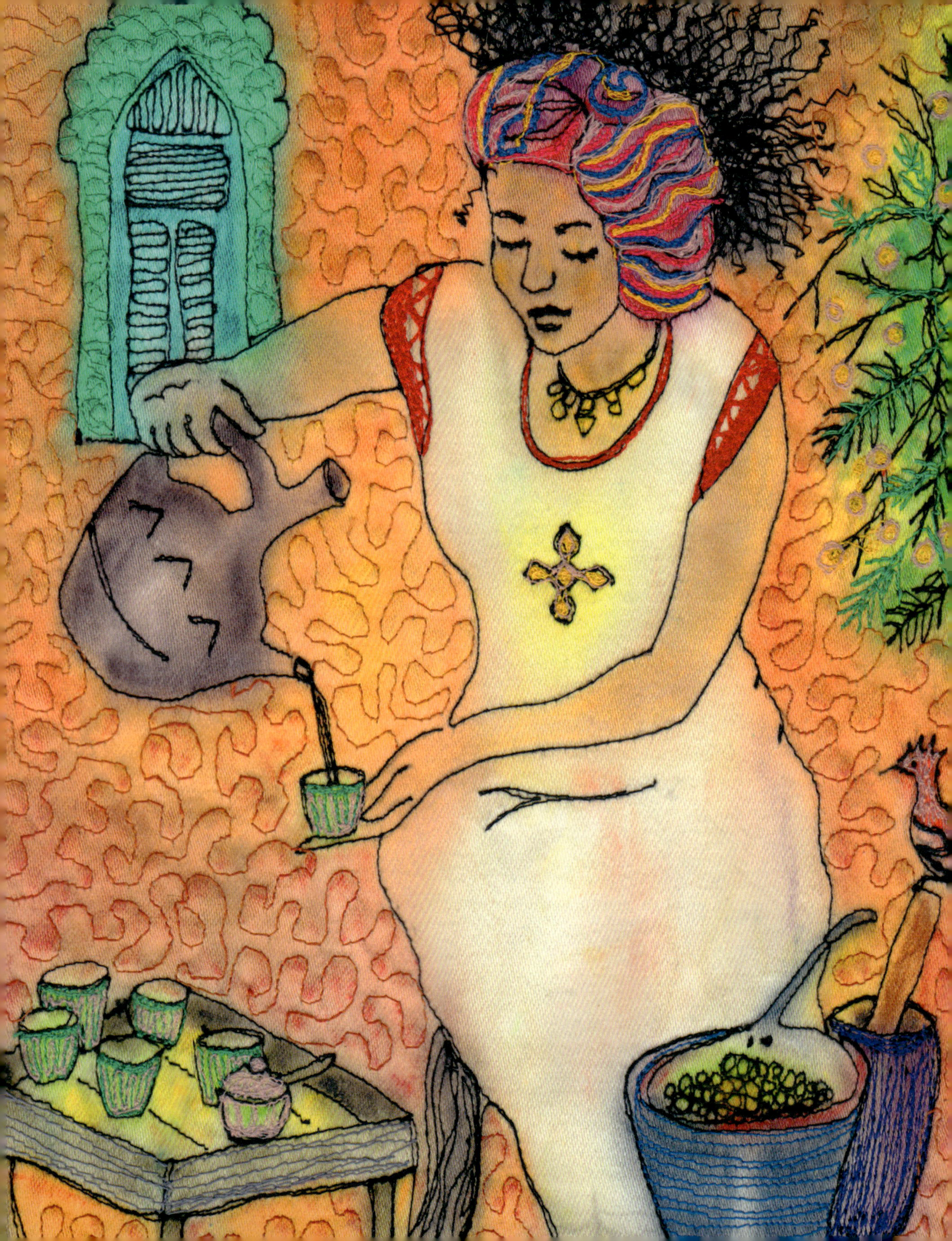

ERITREA

Art by Lydia Fernandez-Arias

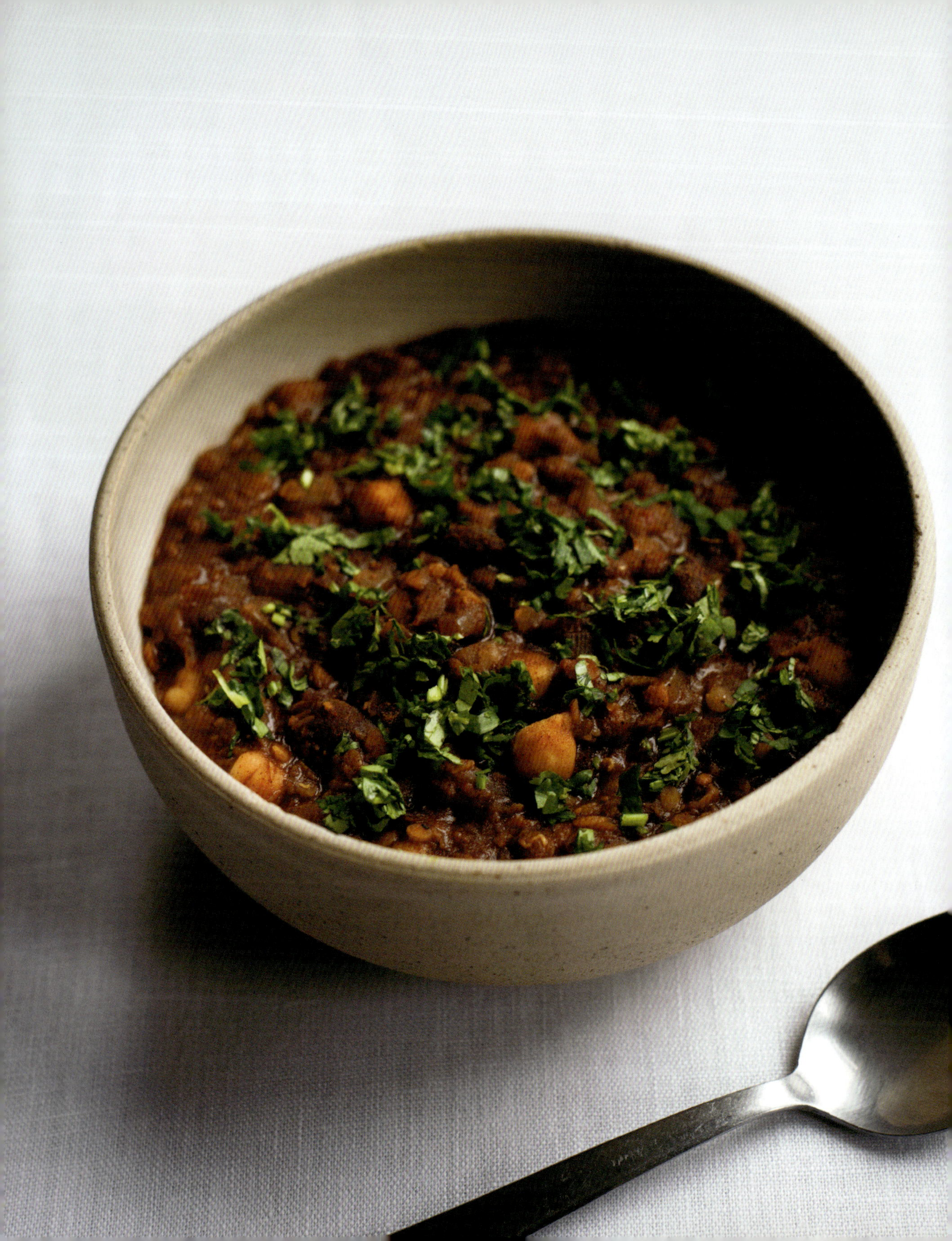

TSEBHI BIRSEN

Serves 6

75 mins

This Eritrean stew is packed full of flavour. Similar to a dahl, it's a great way to use up those lentils hidden at the back of the cupboard!

INGREDIENTS

2 brown onions, diced
3 garlic cloves, crushed
1 thumb-sized piece of ginger, peeled and grated
200g red lentils, washed
400g tin of chopped tomatoes
3 tbsps tomato purée
400g tin of chickpeas, drained and rinsed
400g tin of kidney beans, drained and rinsed
750ml chicken stock
2 tbsps olive oil

FOR THE SPICE MIX

3 tsps paprika
2 tsps cayenne pepper
2 tsps cumin seeds
2 tsps coriander seeds
3 tsps of allspice
1 tsp ground fenugreek
1 tsp ground cinnamon
1 tsp ground nutmeg
6 cardamom pods, burst and shells discarded
½ tsp ground black pepper

METHOD

1. Begin by making the spice mix. Dry fry the cumin and coriander seeds in a pan over a medium heat for 1 minute. Transfer the seeds to a pestle and mortar together with the contents of the cardamom pods, then crush. Add the other spices, mix, then leave to one side.

2. Add the olive oil to a large pan over a medium heat. Add the onions and a pinch of salt then cook for 10 minutes or until soft, stirring throughout.

3. Next add the garlic and ginger. Cook for a further 2 minutes.

4. Reduce to a low heat then add the spice mix. Combine and cook for 5 minutes, stirring constantly to ensure the spices don't burn.

5. Add the stock, lentils, chopped tomatoes and tomato purée then raise the heat to a simmer. Put the lid on and reduce to a low heat. Cook for 30 minutes or until the lentils are soft. Stir occasionally and add a dash of water to prevent the stew from sticking to the base of the pan.

6. Add the chickpeas and kidney beans. Cook for a final 5 minutes then serve.

Chef's tips

Cook slowly on a low heat to maintain the aromatic flavours.
Serve with yoghurt and flat breads.
VEGAN SWITCH Use vegan-friendly vegetable stock.

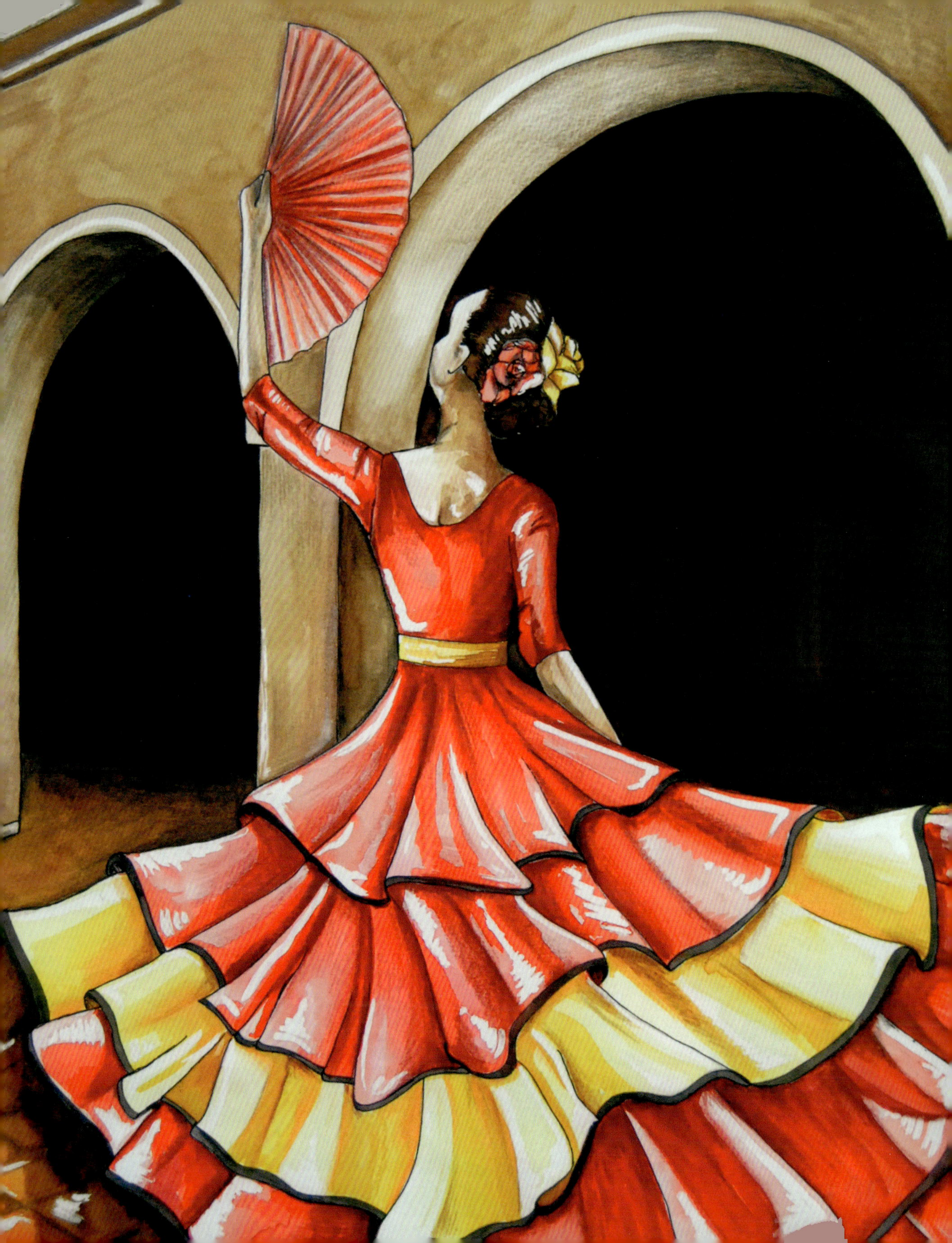

SPAIN

Art by Victoria Rebekah

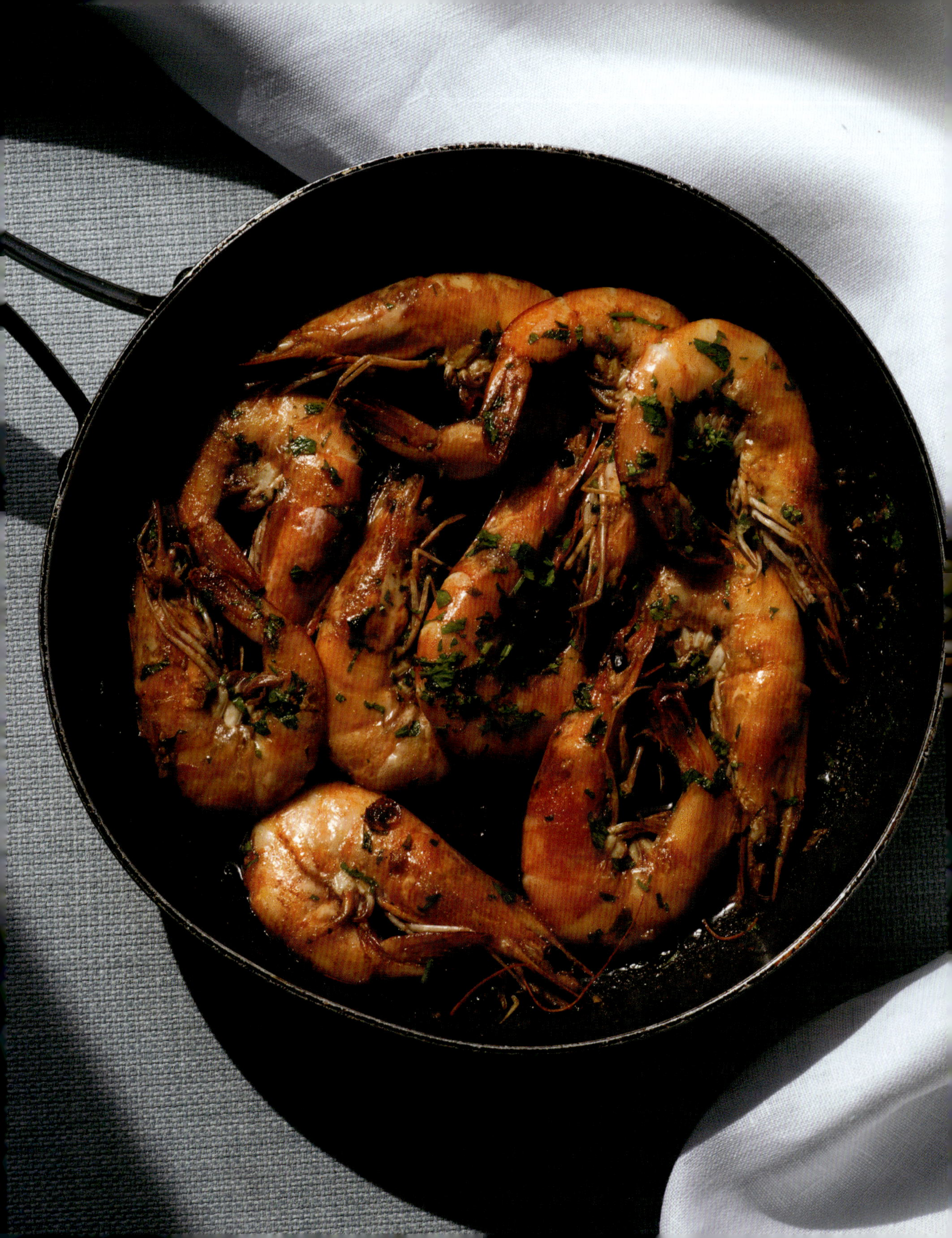

GAMBAS AL AJILLO

Serves 6 | 30 mins

A real tapas classic that is guaranteed to please!

INGREDIENTS

- 10 tiger prawns
- 3 garlic cloves, crushed
- 1 red chilli, deseeded and finely chopped
- Handful of fresh parsley, finely chopped
- 50g butter
- 2 tsps smoked paprika
- Juice of 1 lemon
- 3 tbsps olive oil
- Salt to taste

METHOD

1. Add the olive oil and butter to a large pan over a medium heat and melt together.
2. Add the garlic, chilli, smoked paprika and a pinch of salt. Cook for 2 minutes.
3. Add the prawns and cook for 3 minutes or until fully cooked.
4. Mix in the parsley, cover in fresh lemon juice and serve.

Chef's tips

Use some bread to soak up all the tasty chilli butter.
All types of prawns will work with this dish, vary the quantity to your preference.
VEGAN SWITCH Replace the prawns with pan-fried tofu and use vegan butter instead.

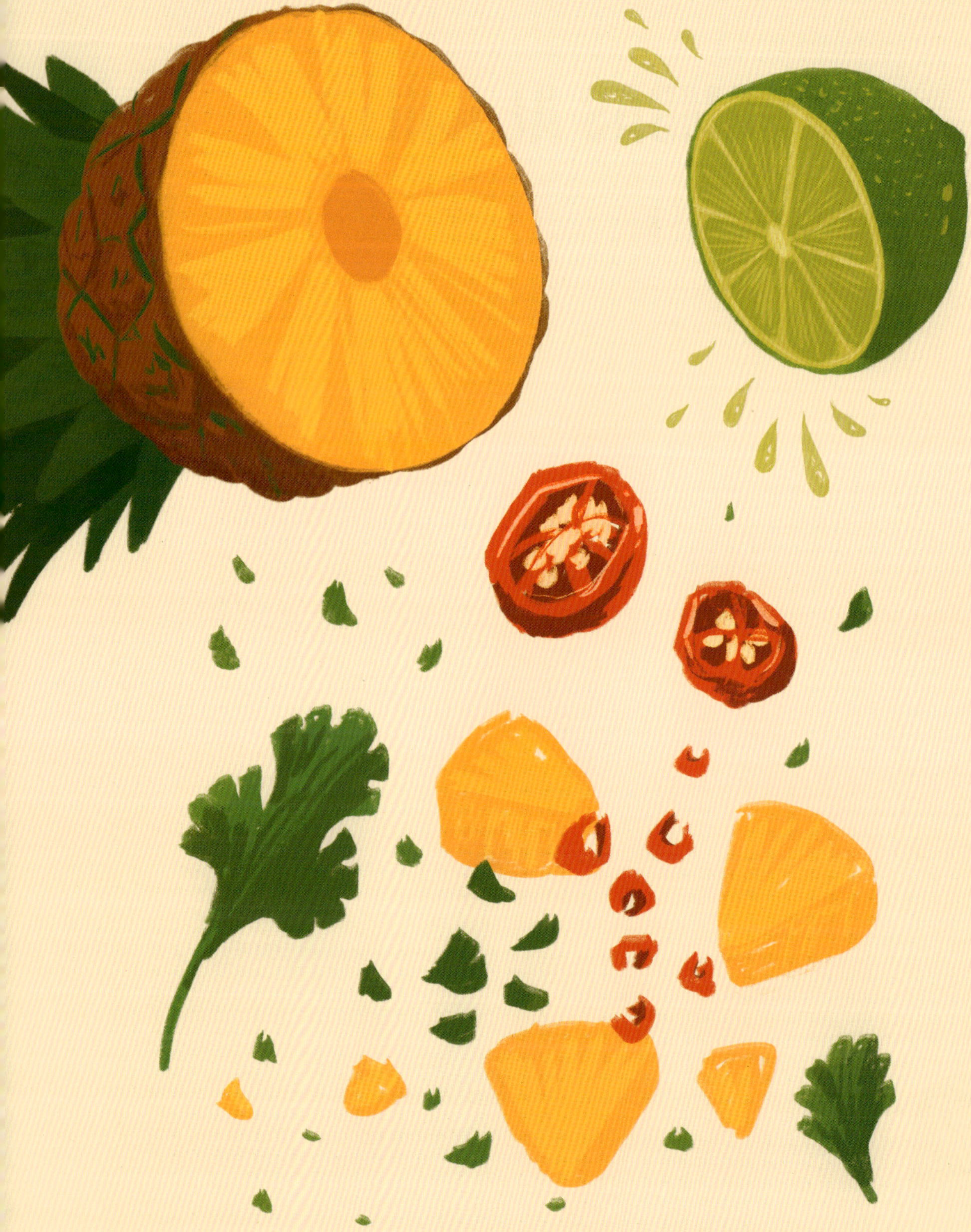

TRINIDAD & TOBAGO

Art by Emma Reynolds

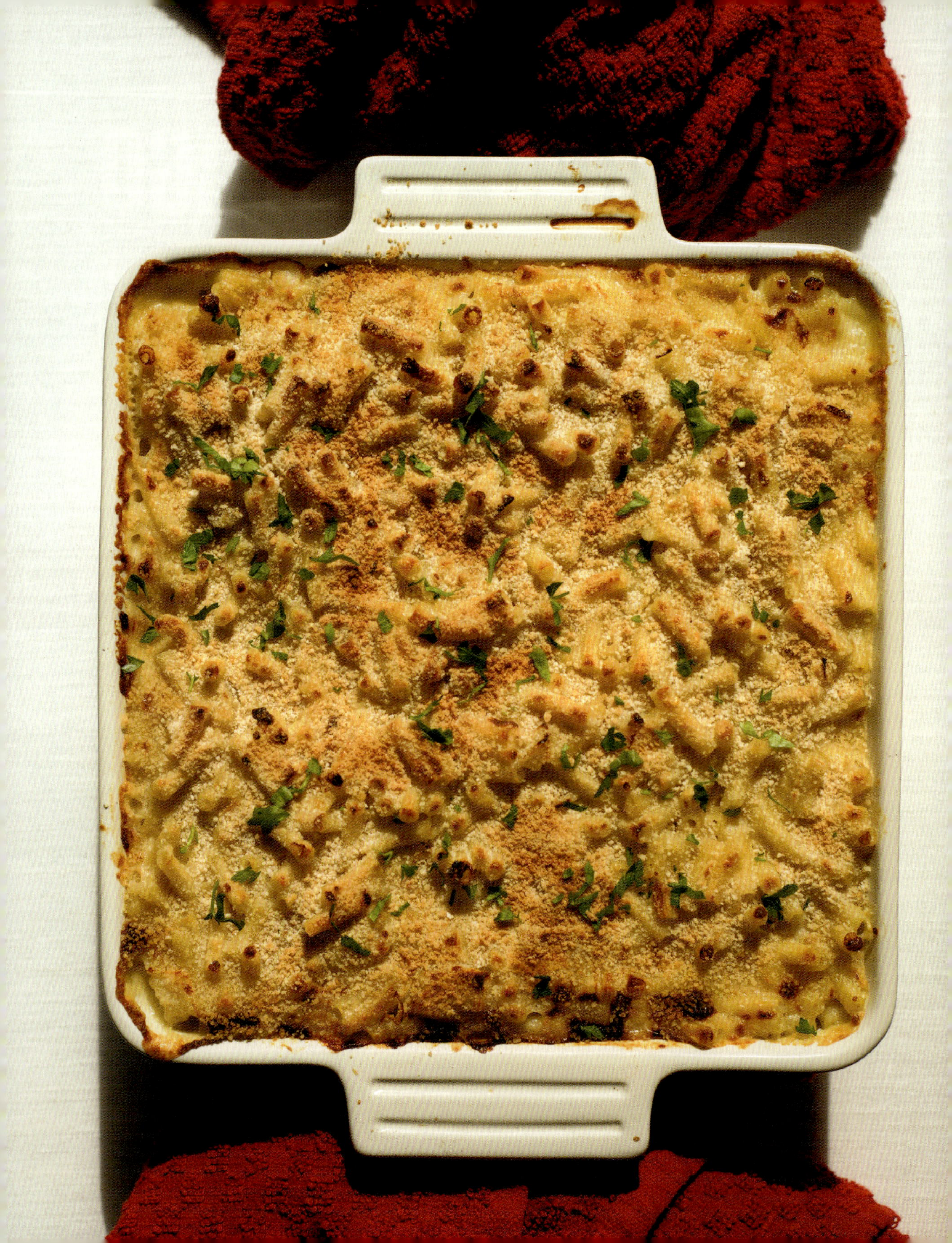

MAC & CHEESE

Serves 4-6 | 45 mins | Vegetarian

This dish is especially popular in the Caribbean where it is often served with a roast and sometimes known as Mac & Cheese Pie.

INGREDIENTS

500g macaroni
50g butter
30g plain flour
600ml milk
300g cheddar cheese, grated
1 brown onion, diced
4 tbsps dried breadcrumbs
Salt to taste
Handful of fresh parsley, chopped (optional)
Smoked paprika (optional)
1 egg (optional)

METHOD

1. Pre-heat the oven to 180°C.
2. Place the macaroni in a pan and fill with boiling water. Add a pinch of salt, bring to the boil and cook for 10 minutes.
3. While you wait for the pasta, melt half the butter in a large pan over a medium heat. Add the onions, then cook for 5 minutes or until soft.
4. Strain the pasta then combine with the onions in a deep baking tray and leave to one side.
5. Return to the pan you cooked the onions in and melt the remaining butter over a low heat.
6. Once melted, begin to sieve in the flour a bit at a time, mixing as you go to ensure that no clumps remain. A flat spatula works well as a mixing tool to prevent the sauce sticking to the pan.
7. Once all the flour has been added start pouring in the milk, again a little bit at a time, mixing as you go. Continue this process until you have created a sauce of enough volume to cover the pasta and of a consistency to your liking.
8. Add the cheese, a handful at a time, until it has all melted in the sauce. Pour this over the pasta in the baking tray and mix evenly.
9. Sprinkle breadcrumbs on top of the pasta then cover with tin foil. Place in the oven for 10 minutes.
10. Remove the tin foil and finish under the grill for two minutes on a medium heat.

Chef's tips

Top with olive oil, fresh parsley or a dusting of smoked paprika for a final flourish!
To make a more authentic Trinidadian Mac & Cheese Pie, add a beaten egg into the mixture before placing in the oven.
VEGAN SWITCH Use vegan butter, cheese and almond or oat milk instead.

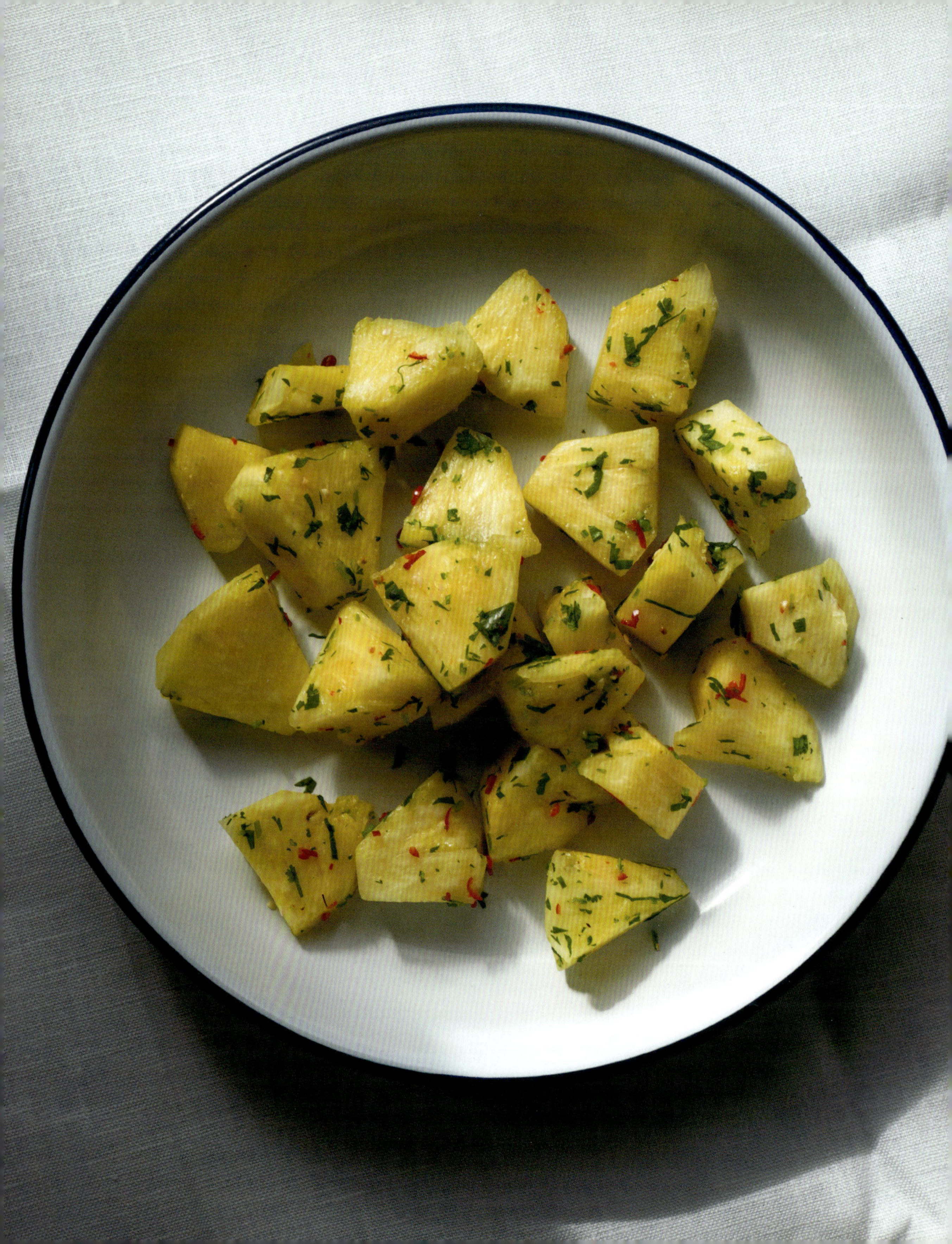

PINEAPPLE CHOW

Serves 6 | 20 mins | Vegan

This fresh, tasty pineapple salad also has a spicy kick.

INGREDIENTS

1 pineapple, cut into chunks

Handful of fresh coriander, finely chopped

2 red chillies, finely chopped

Juice of 2 limes

METHOD

1. Mix all ingredients in a large bowl.
2. Taste and adjust seasoning to your preference!

Chef's tips

Adjust the ingredient quantities to create your perfect flavour combination! Take care when cutting the pineapple by using a sharp chef's knife.

MALI
AFRICA
REPUBLIQUE DU MALI
POSTES 80F
TALA
AGRICULTURE
POSTES
REPUBLIQUE DU MALI
ARTISANAT
REPUBLIQUE DU MALI

MALI

Art by James Blinkhorn

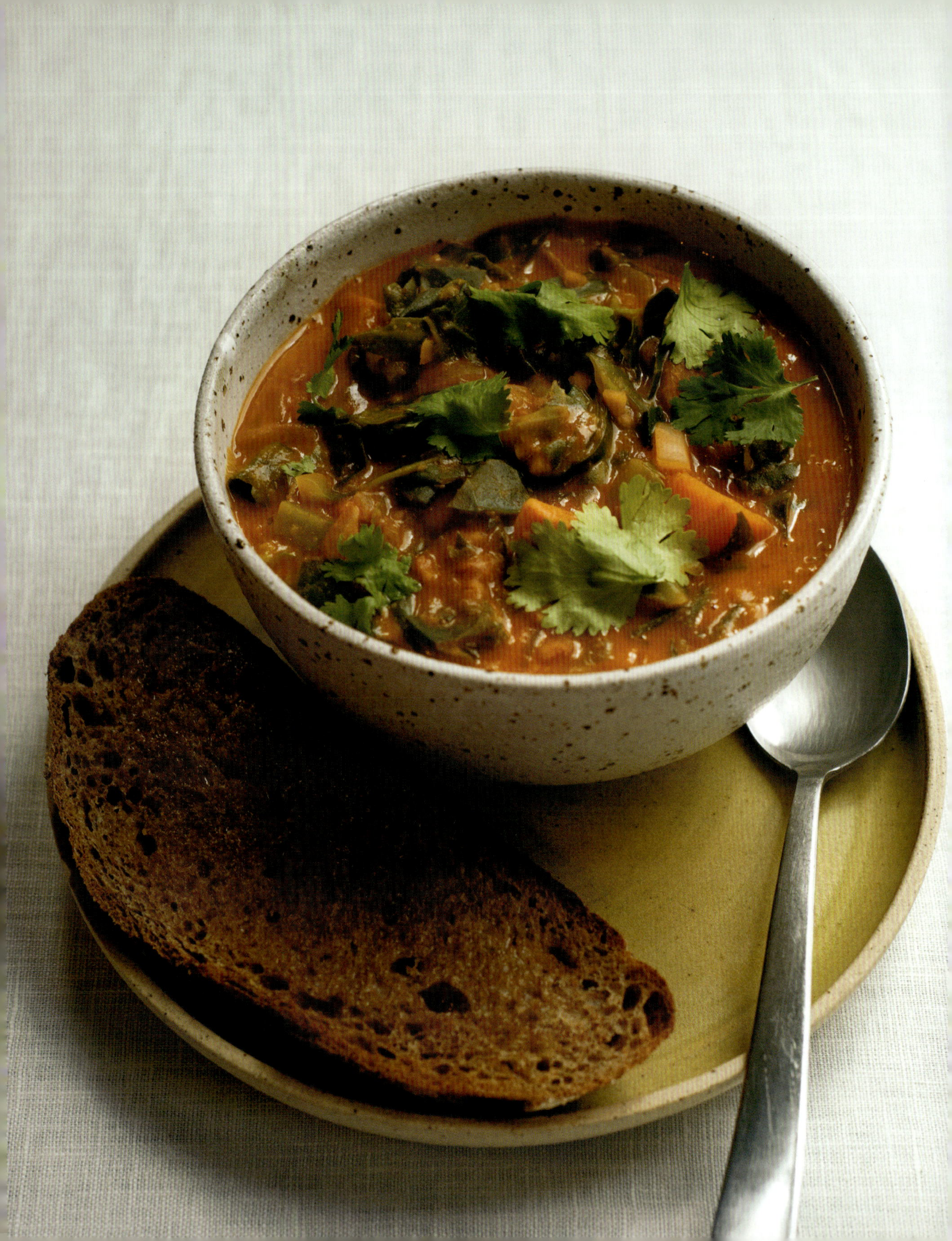

MAAFE

Serves 4-5 | 45 mins | Vegetarian

This rich peanut stew is popular throughout West Africa and is traditionally made with chicken or beef.

INGREDIENTS

- 2 medium sweet potatoes, peeled and diced
- 300g spring greens, roughly chopped
- 2 brown onions, diced
- 2 tbsps vegetable oil
- 3 tbsps tomato purée
- 1 green chilli, finely chopped
- 3 garlic cloves, crushed
- 1 thumb-sized piece of ginger, peeled and grated
- 300g peanut butter
- 2 tsps ground cumin
- ½ tsp cayenne pepper
- 1 litre vegetable stock
- Handful of fresh coriander, finely chopped (optional)

METHOD

1. Add the vegetable oil to a large pan over a medium heat. Add the onions then fry for 5 minutes or until soft.
2. Add the garlic, ginger and chilli. Cook for a further 2 minutes.
3. Lower the heat then add the tomato purée, cumin and cayenne pepper mixing thoroughly for an even consistency.
4. Add the sweet potato and cook for 5 minutes, stirring throughout.
5. Add the stock and allow to cook for 15 minutes or until the the sweet potato is soft.
6. Add the spring greens and cook for a further 2 minutes.
7. Finish by adding the peanut butter 1 tablespoon at a time. Mix to ensure there is a smooth consistency.

Chef's tips

Freshly chopped coriander works well as an optional garnish on top.
VEGAN SWITCH Use vegan-friendly vegetable stock.

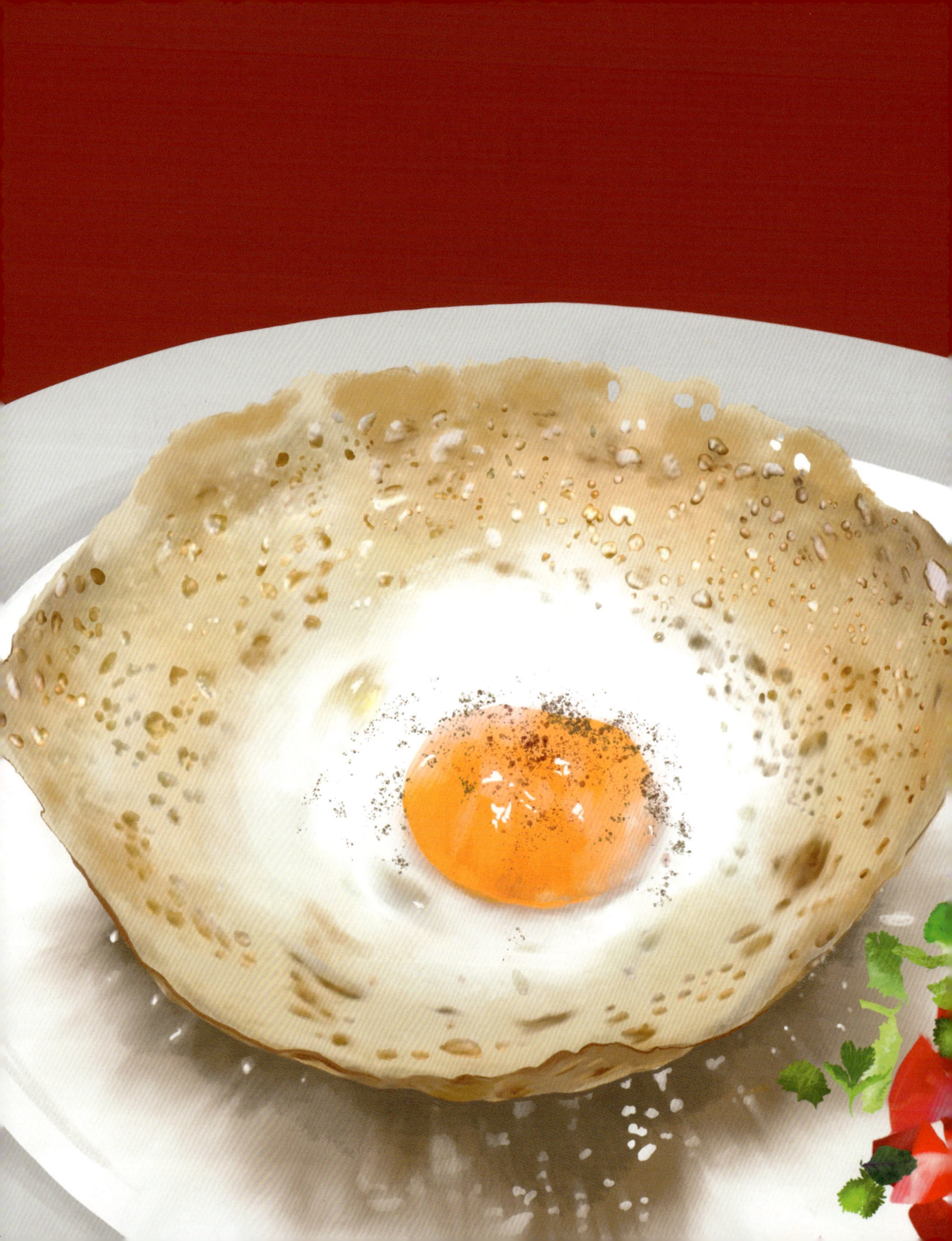

SRI LANKA

Art by Alexandra Boocock

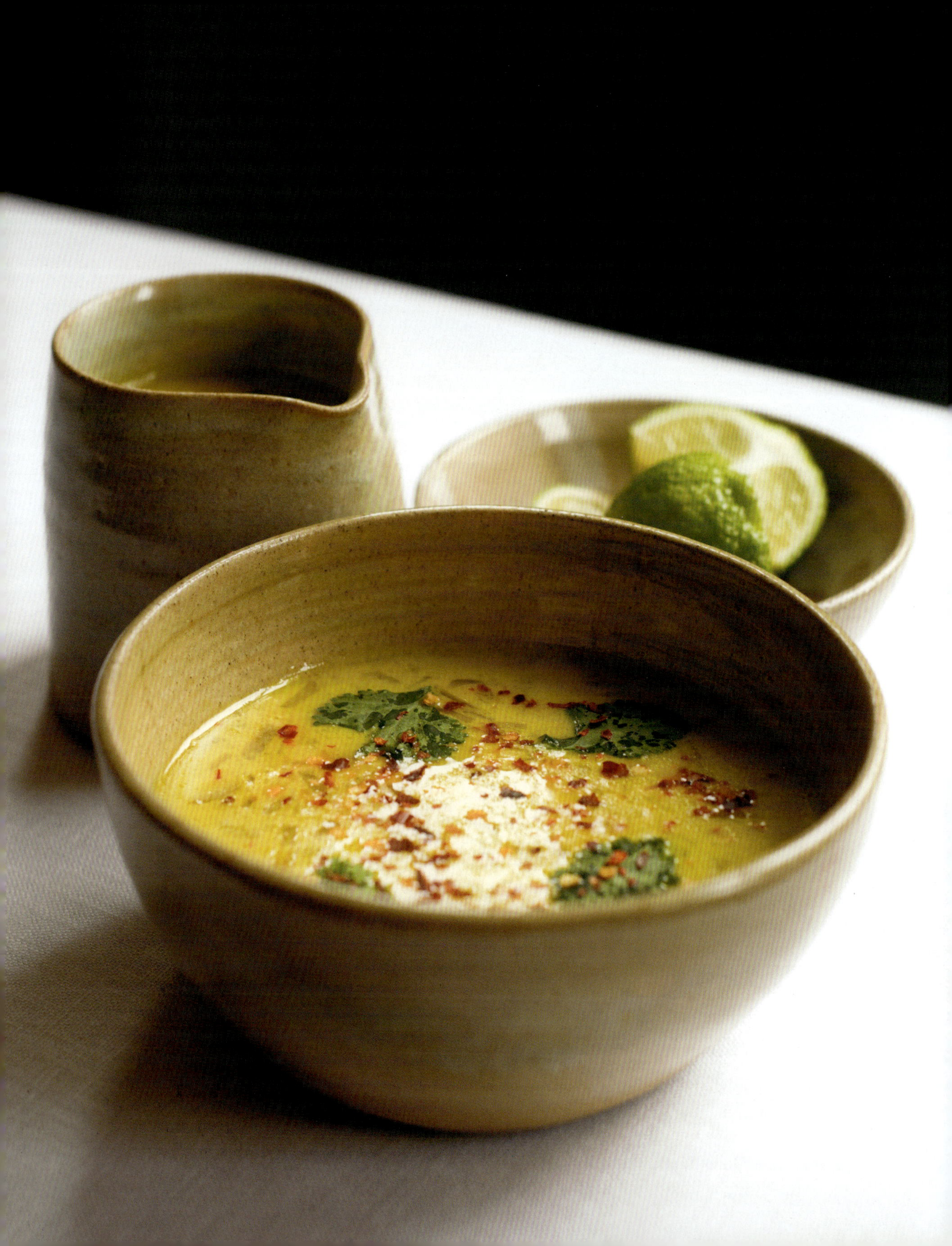

KIRI HODI

Serves 4-6 | 40 mins | Vegan

This aromatic coconut gravy pairs beautifully with egg appam for an exciting Sri Lankan brunch!

INGREDIENTS

1 tsp ground fenugreek
1 tsp coriander seeds
1½ tsps turmeric
1 cinnamon stick
2 star anise
400ml tin of coconut milk
1 brown onion, sliced
3 garlic cloves, crushed
½ tsp dried chilli flakes
Juice of 1 lime
2 tbsps vegetable oil
Salt to taste
Handful of fresh coriander, finely chopped (optional)

METHOD

1. Dry fry the coriander seeds in a pan over a medium heat for 1 minute. Transfer the seeds to a pestle and mortar then crush. Combine with the fenugreek, chilli flakes, turmeric, cinnamon stick and star anise then leave to one side.

2. Add the vegetable oil to a large pan over a medium heat. Add the onions and a pinch of salt then cook for 10 minutes or until soft, stirring throughout.

3. Add the garlic and cook for a further 2 minutes.

4. Reduce to a low heat then add the spice mix. Combine and cook for 2 minutes, stirring constantly to ensure the spices don't burn.

5. Add the coconut milk and lime juice. Cook for a final 10 minutes, stirring occasionally.

Chef's tips

For a more authentic flavour add several curry leaves.
Freshly chopped coriander works well as an optional garnish on top.

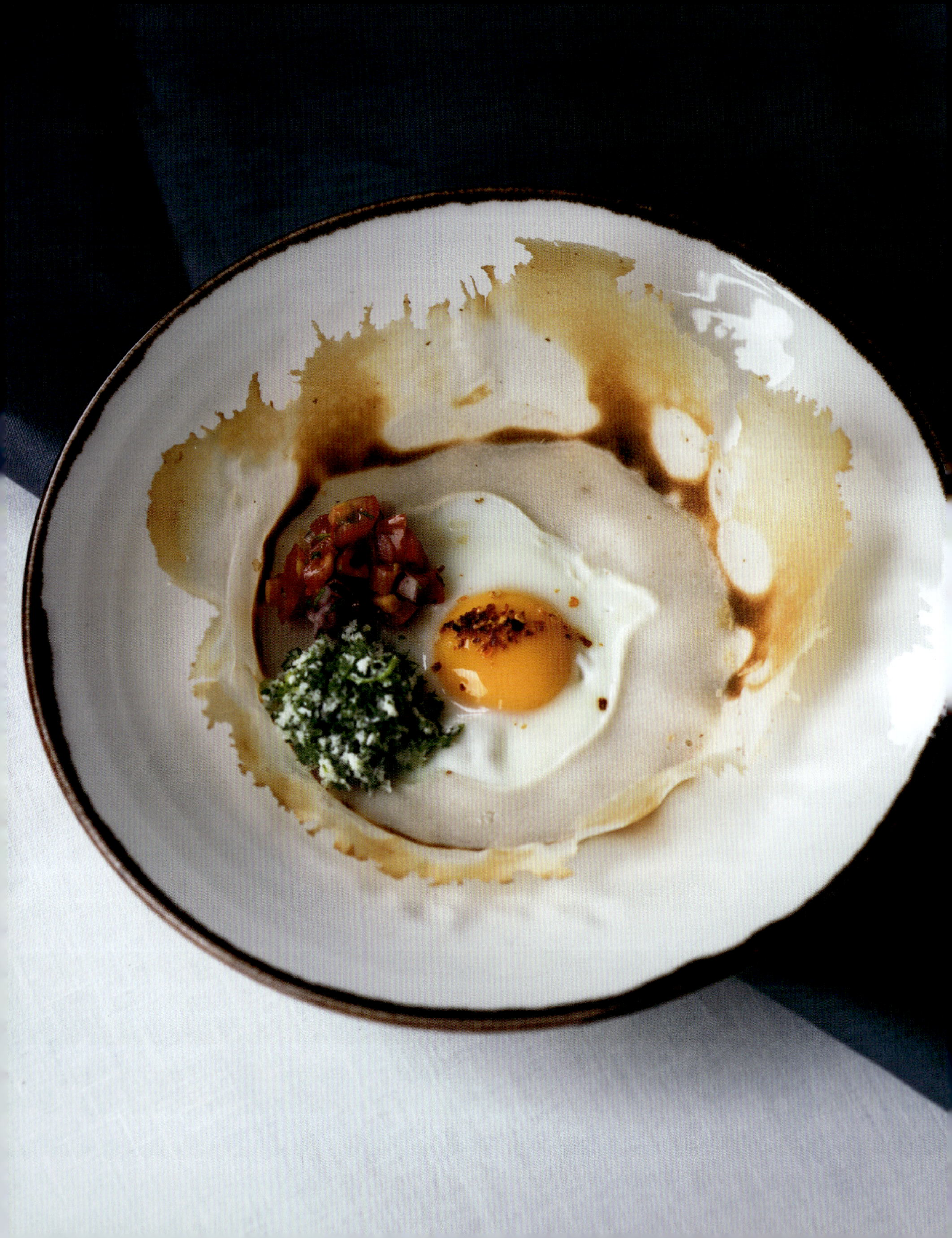

EGG APPAM

Serves 4-6 | 60 mins | Vegetarian

Egg Appam are a Sri Lankan staple. They were traditionally made in bowl-shaped appa pans, hence their name and distinctive shape!

INGREDIENTS

360g rice flour
800ml coconut milk
1½ tsps yeast
3 tsps sugar
1 egg per person

METHOD

1. Start by making the batter. Mix the yeast and sugar in a small container with a dash of water and leave to one side for 10 minutes.
2. Sieve the flour into a large mixing bowl.
3. Add the yeast and sugar solution to the flour and mix evenly.
4. Slowly add the coconut milk and mix with a whisk until a consistent batter forms.
5. Cover the batter with cling film then pierce using a fork to allow the mixture to breathe. Leave to stand for 20 minutes.
6. Heat a non-stick frying pan over a medium heat.
7. Ladle one portion of batter into the pan. Tilt and rotate to spread the mixture evenly.
8. Lower the heat slightly, then crack an egg into the centre of the pan on top of the batter. Fry for a further 5 minutes or until the egg is cooked to your preference. Use a spatula to get underneath and turn the pancake as it cooks.

chef's tips

For a traditional fermented flavour, leave the batter to stand overnight.
Using a small wok will give you the traditional bowl-shaped appam, however a normal frying pan will also suffice.
Getting these right takes practice and depends on a number of factors including the depth of batter, heat of the pan and type of spatula you're using.
VEGAN SWITCH Omit the eggs.

BUENOS AIRES

ARGENTINA

Art by Peter Lang

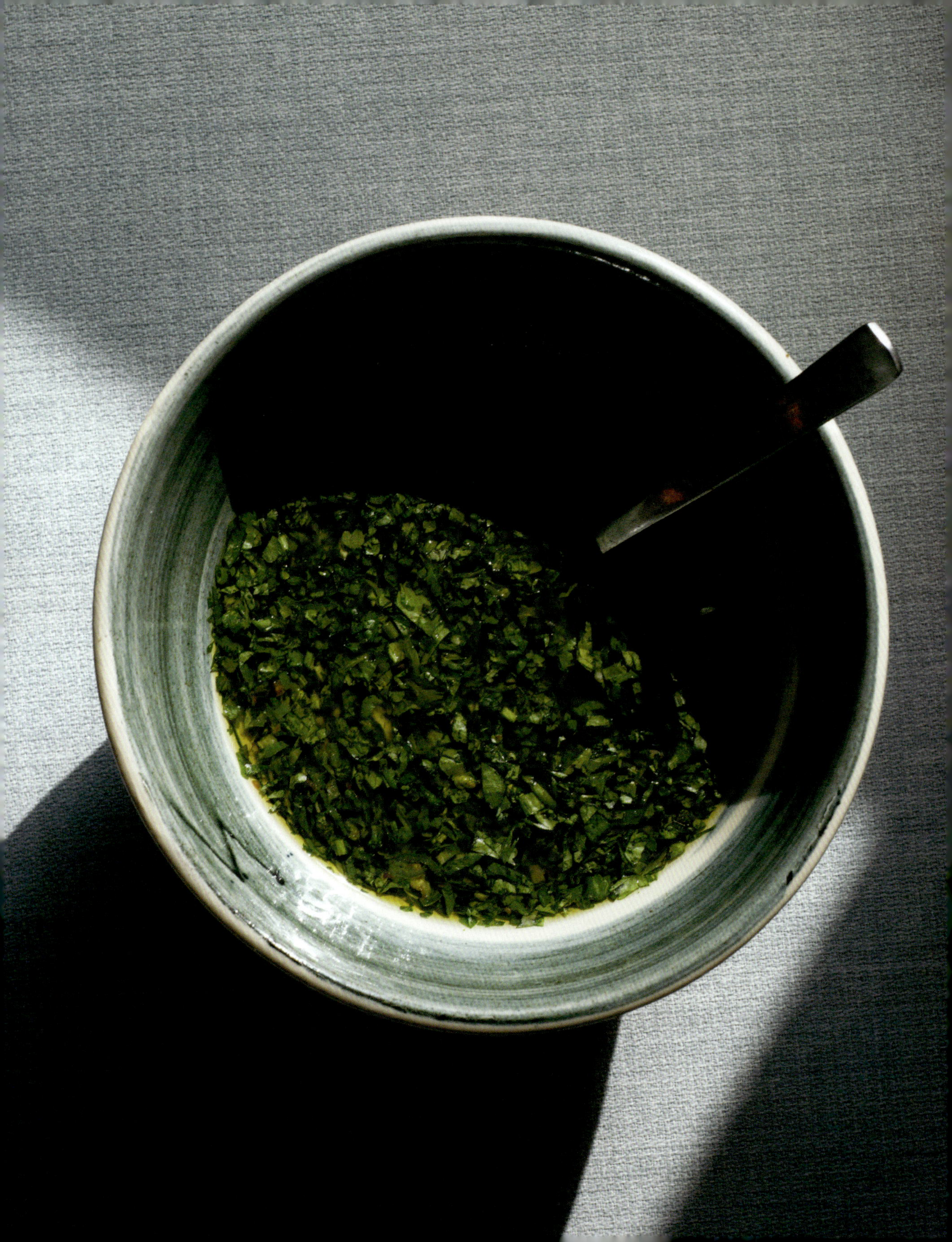

CHIMICHURI

Serves 4-6 | **20 mins** | **Vegan**

This classic condiment traditionally accompanies beef but also adds an extra dimension to a range of vegetarian and vegan dishes.

INGREDIENTS

- 35g fresh parsley, finely chopped
- 15g fresh coriander, finely chopped
- 15g fresh oregano, finely chopped
- 4 garlic cloves, crushed
- 250ml olive oil
- Juice of ½ lemon
- 3 green chillies, finely chopped

METHOD

1. Mix all ingredients in a large bowl.
2. Taste and adjust seasoning to your preference!

Chef's tips: Adjust the ingredient quantities to create your perfect flavour combination!

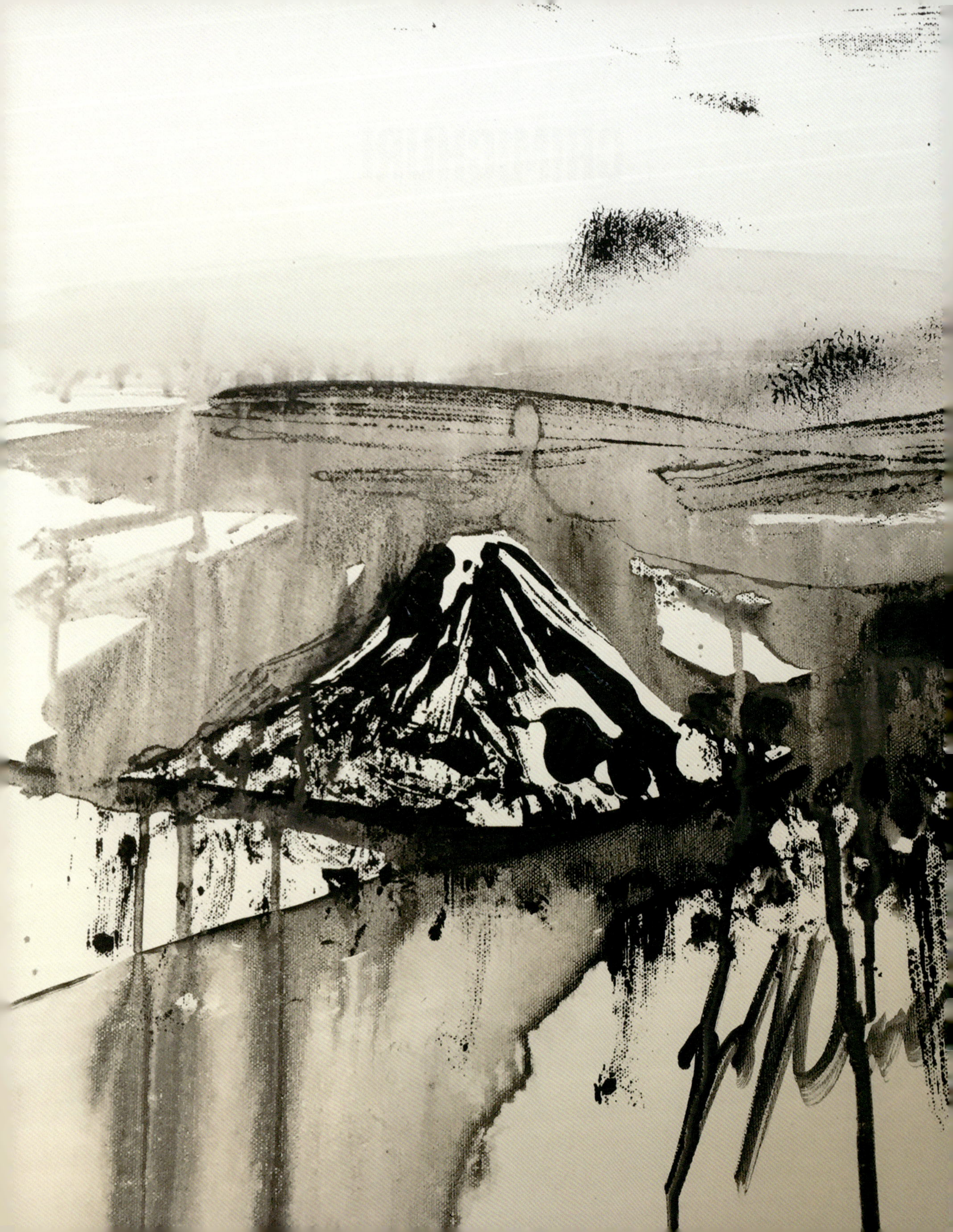

JAPAN

Art by Jessica Owen

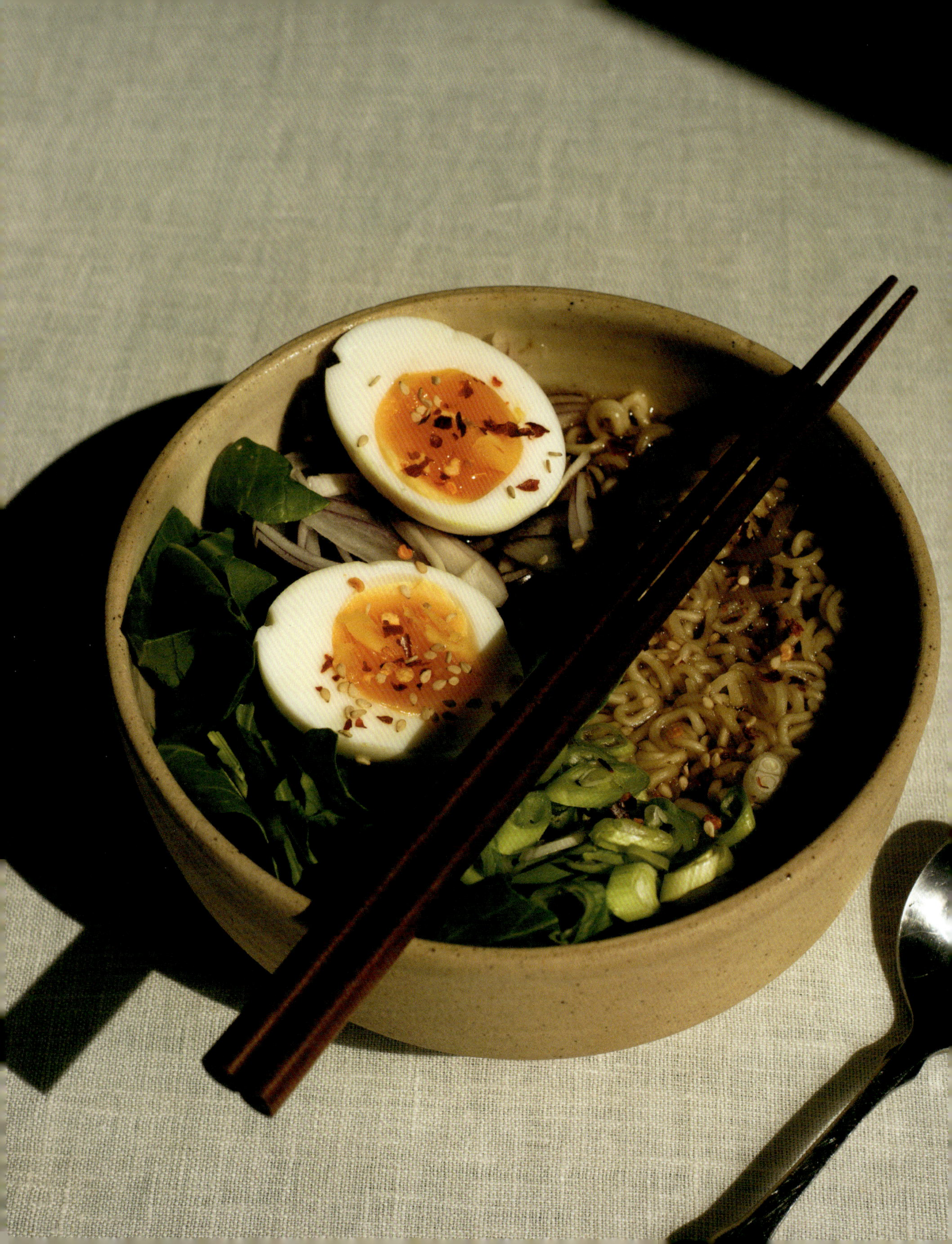

RAMEN

Serves 4-6 | 45 mins | Vegetarian

Ramen is a staple Japanese soup that can be made in a number of ways. This vegetable version is full of flavour and straightforward to make!

INGREDIENTS

FOR THE SOUP

2 litres vegetable stock
1 brown onion, sliced
200g ramen noodles
4 tsps miso paste
2 tsps Chinese five spice
½ tsp dried chilli flakes
8 tsps light soy sauce
2 tsps sesame oil
1 thumb-sized piece of ginger, peeled and thinly sliced
4 garlic cloves, thinly sliced

TOPPING OPTIONS

1 boiled egg, peeled and halved
1 red onion, sliced
40g spring onions, thinly sliced
2 pak choi, sliced
Sesame seeds

METHOD

1. Add the vegetable stock to a large pan and bring to the boil.
2. Reduce the heat to a simmer then add the garlic, ginger, brown onion, miso paste, soy sauce, sesame oil, chilli flakes and Chinese five spice. Cook for at least 20 minutes while the flavours infuse.
3. In a separate pan cover your noodles in boiling water and cook for 5 minutes or until soft.
4. Strain the cooked noodles then portion them into the number of serving bowls required.
5. Make sure the ramen is piping hot, then use a ladle to cover each bowl of noodles with soup.
6. Cover your ramen with a combination of the suggested toppings and serve.

Chef's tips

Note that the red onion, spring onion and pak choi toppings can either be added to your ramen raw or fried, depending on your preference.
VEGAN SWITCH Omit the egg and use vegan-friendly vegetable stock and noodles.

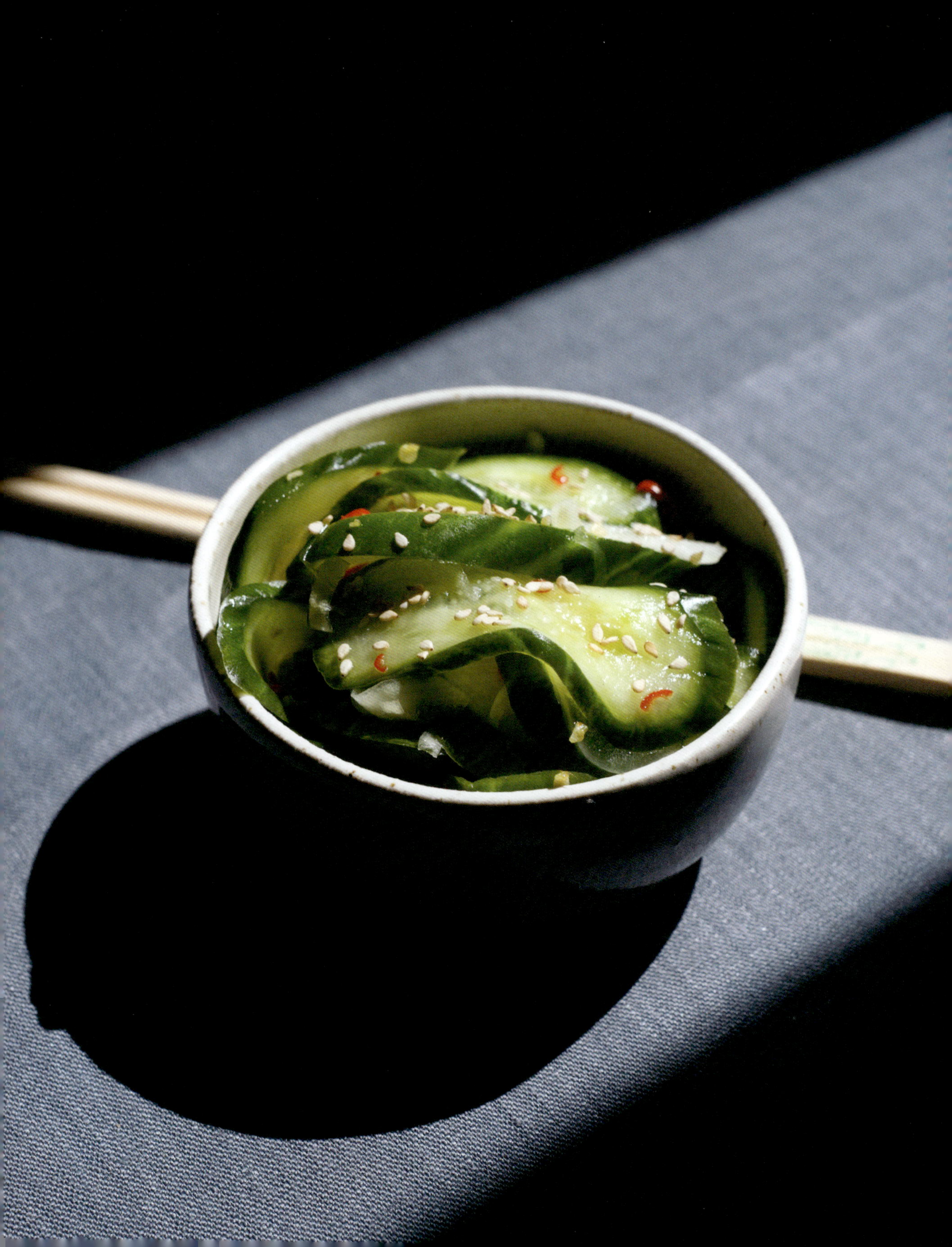

TSUKEMONO

Serves 4-6 | 45 mins +60 mins marinating | Vegan

This is a traditional Japanese pickle with plenty of tang! It works well as a side or as part of several small plates.

INGREDIENTS

1 cucumber, sliced into thin discs
1 red chilli, deseeded and finely chopped
2 tsps sesame seeds
½ brown onion, sliced
150ml rice vinegar
2 ½ tbsps salt
4 tsps sugar

METHOD

1. Add the cucumber and onion to a large mixing bowl then cover evenly with salt.
2. Fill a smaller second bowl with cold water. Place this directly on top of the cucumbers and onions then leave for 30 minutes while the weight of the bowl and salt help to remove excess water from the vegetables.
3. Remove the bowl of water then strain the vegetables in a colander before adding them back into the large mixing bowl.
4. Add the sugar, chilli and vinegar. Mix until the sugar dissolves then leave for at least 1 hour to marinate.
5. Strain and discard any excess liquid. Top with the sesame seeds and serve.

Chef's tips

Adding black and white sesame seeds really adds to the presentation!
Speed up the process of removing excess water from the vegetables in step 2 by applying pressure to the bowl of water on top of them.

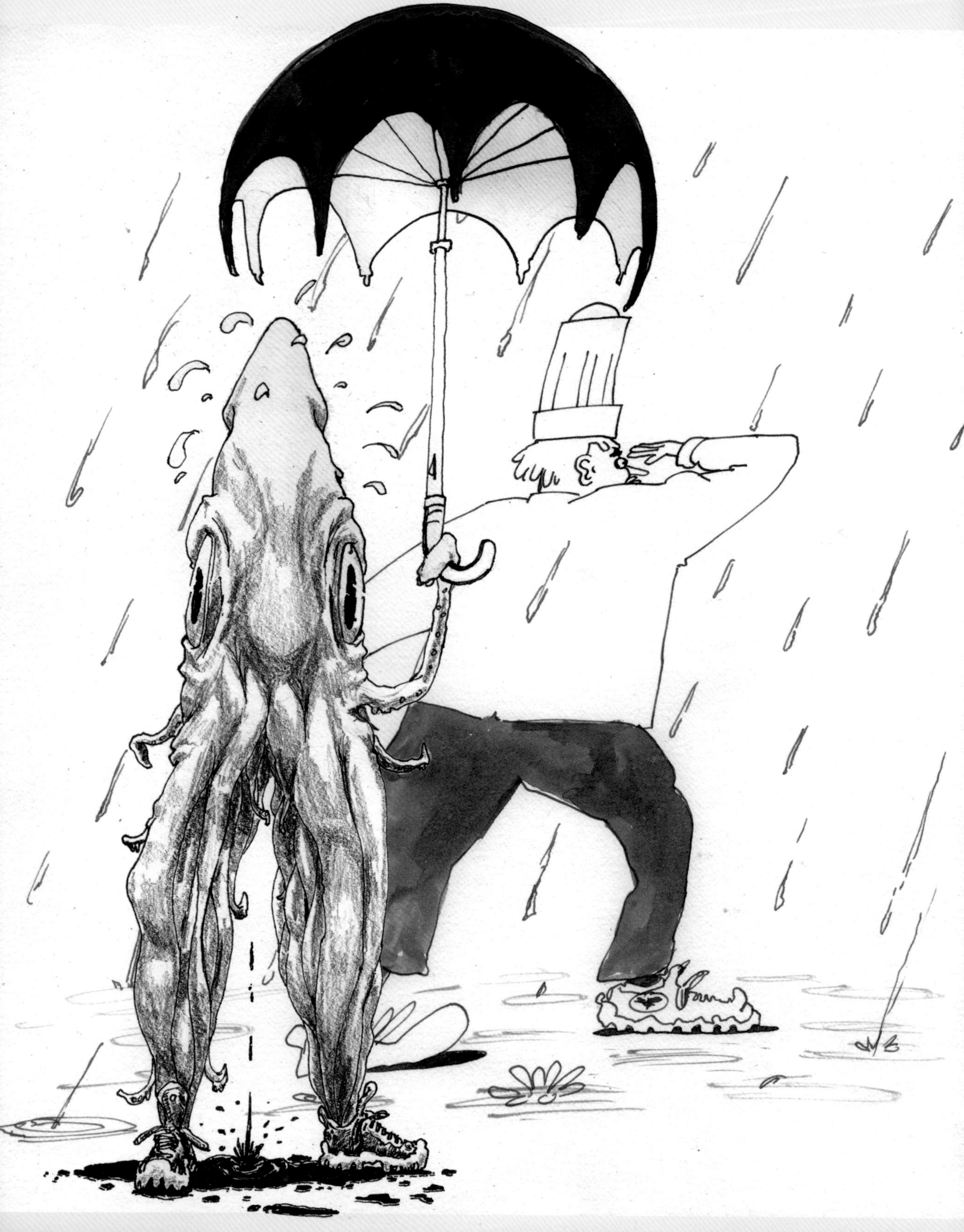

PHILIPPINES

Art by Rory Spencer

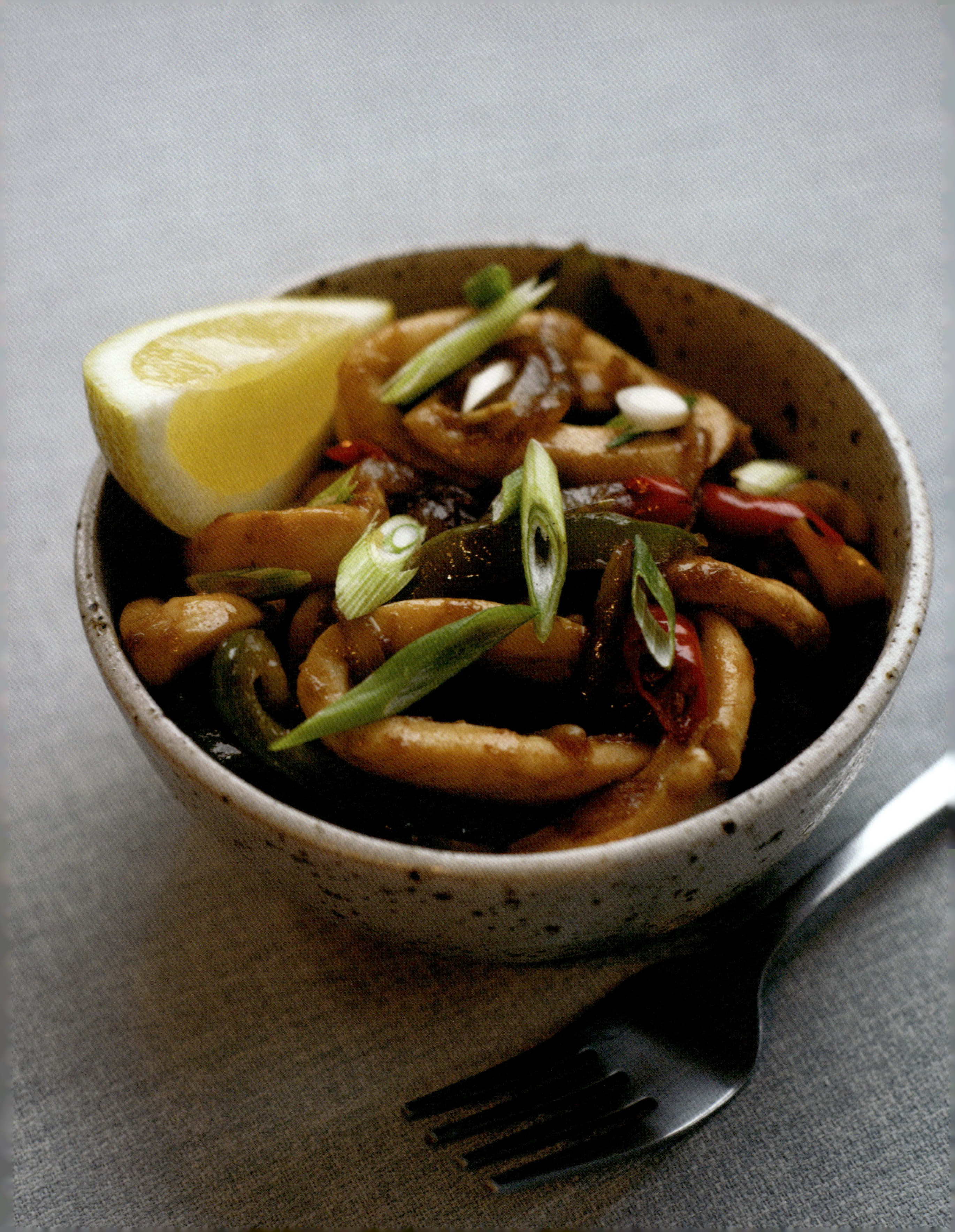

SISIG NA PUSIT

Serves 3   **40 mins**

Sour, salty and full of spice, this dish is a must try for seafood lovers!

INGREDIENTS

500g squid, cleaned and sliced into to rings

1 brown onion, sliced

70g spring onions, sliced

½ bell pepper, sliced

3 red chillies, chopped into thirds

3 garlic cloves, crushed

1 thumb-sized piece of ginger, peeled and grated

2 lemons, 1 juiced and 1 cut into wedges

3 tbsps light soy sauce

3 tbsps red wine vinegar

3 tbsps oyster sauce

1 tsp sesame oil

1 tbsp vegetable oil

Salt to taste

Rice (optional)

METHOD

1. Combine the juice of 1 lemon, soy sauce, oyster sauce, sesame oil, red wine vinegar, ginger and garlic in a large bowl and mix thoroughly.

2. Add the vegetable oil to a large frying pan over a medium heat. Add the brown onion and cook for 5 minutes or until soft.

3. Add the pepper and chillies. Cook for 2 minutes.

4. Add the garlic and ginger. Cook for a further 2 minutes.

5. Add the squid rings to the frying pan. Cook for 5 minutes.

6. Pour the sauce mix into the pan a little bit at a time and mix through.

7. Serve piping hot when the squid is cooked. Garnish with a wedge of lemon and sliced spring onions.

Chef's tips

Serve with rice and feel free to use less chilli if you are averse to heat!

VEGAN SWITCH Use fine green beans instead of squid. Replace the oyster sauce with extra soy sauce and red wine vinegar.

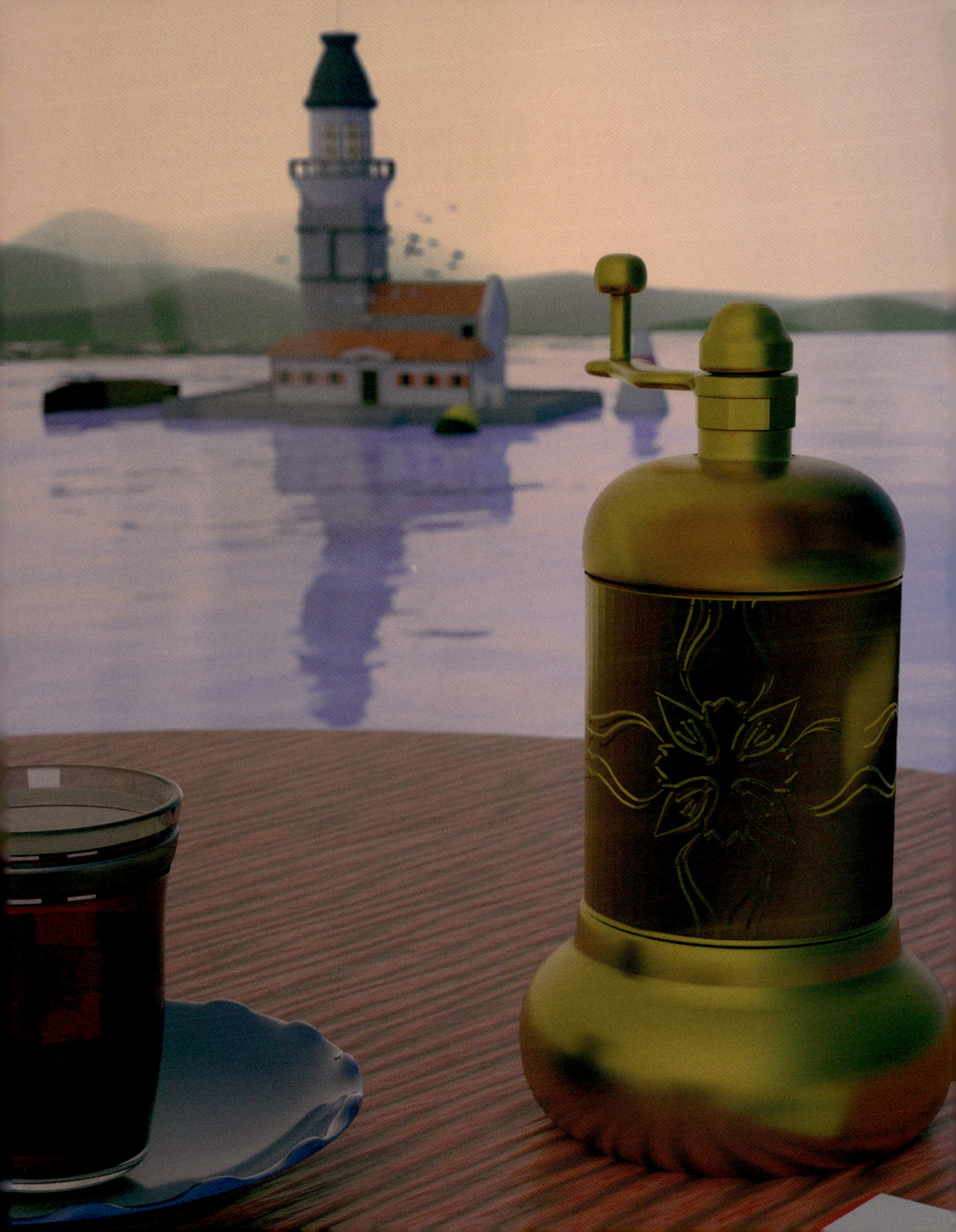

TURKEY

Art by Jamie Griffiths

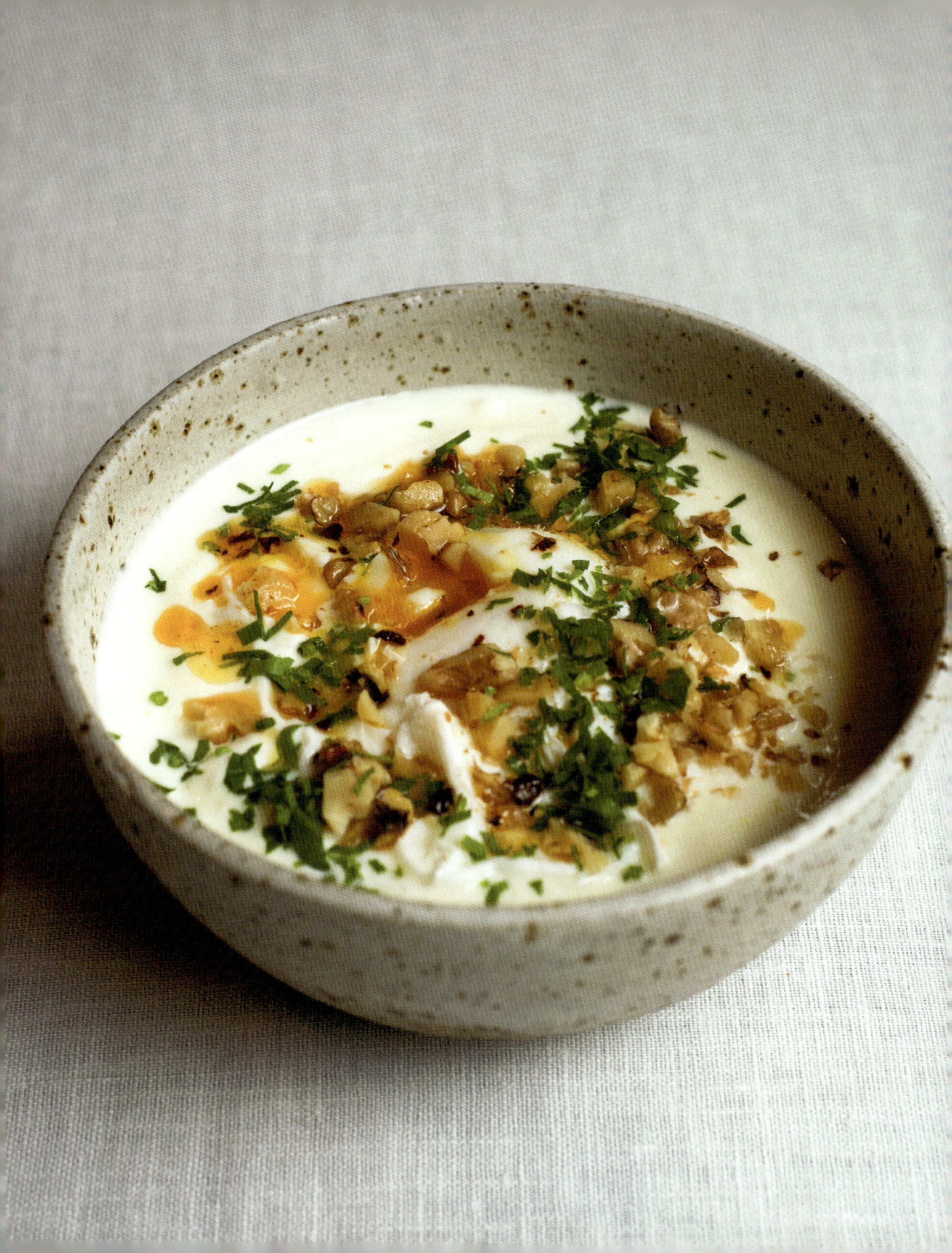

ÇILBIR

Serves 6 | **45 mins** | **Vegetarian**

This classic Turkish dish works well as a light brunch or as part of an evening meal.

INGREDIENTS

500ml Greek yoghurt
6 garlic cloves, crushed
75ml olive oil
80g butter
100g walnuts, roughly chopped
2 tsps chilli flakes
4 eggs
4 slices of wholemeal bread
Handful of fresh parsley, finely chopped
1 tbsp malt vinegar
Salt to taste

METHOD

1. Dry fry the walnuts on a medium heat for 2 minutes or until a light browning appears. Remove from the heat and leave to cool.

2. Melt the butter in a large pan over a medium heat. Continue to heat the butter until it takes on a golden brown colour, this may take 5-10 minutes. When the colour has changed add the chilli flakes and cook for a further 2 minutes.

3. Remove the pan from the heat and carefully strain the butter into a pouring jug with a sieve. Leave to one side to cool.

4. Combine the yoghurt, garlic and olive oil in a large bowl then lightly whip until a smooth, silky consistency forms.

5. Add boiling water to a deep saucepan over a medium heat. Place the bowl of yoghurt above the water and, if possible, try to ensure the bottom of the bowl doesn't touch the surface of the water. The steam will gradually warm the yoghurt, stir slowly throughout to spread the heat. Leave to one side when the mixture reaches room temperature.

6. Add vinegar to the now empty pan of simmering water. Crack your eggs into the pan and poach for 3-6 minutes depending on how runny you want your eggs.

7. Ladle a portion of yoghurt into a bowl. Place your poached egg on top once cooked, then cover with a sprinkling of walnuts and parsley. Drizzle over a dash of the chilli butter and serve with a slice of toast on the side.

Chef's tips

The butter is quite spicy so try a little at first before you cover your portion or reduce the amount of chilli flakes!
VEGAN SWITCH Omit the egg, use vegan butter and plant-based yoghurt instead.

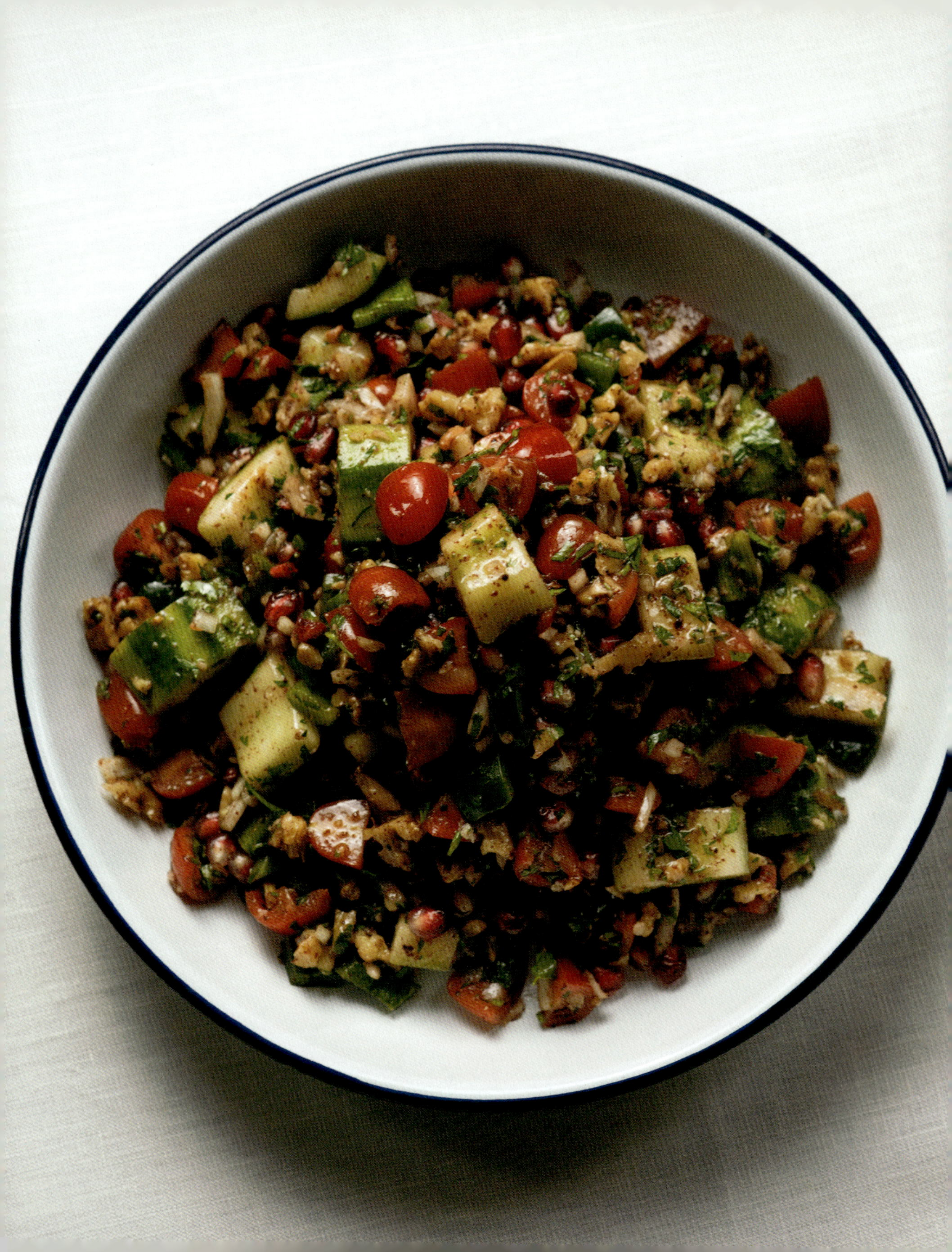

GAVURDAGI SALAD

Serves 6 | **25 mins** | **Vegan**

This fresh and tangy salad originates from the Gaziantep province in south-central Turkey.

INGREDIENTS

- 600g plum tomatoes, cores removed and roughly chopped
- 2 green bell peppers
- 1 white onion, diced
- ½ cucumber, core removed and chopped into chunks
- 100g walnuts, roughly chopped
- 2 garlic cloves, crushed
- Handful of fresh parsley, finely chopped
- ¼ pomegranate, seeds only
- 3 tsps sumac
- 4 tbsps olive oil
- 1 tbsp pomegranate molasses
- Juice of half a lemon
- Salt to taste
- Feta cheese (optional)

METHOD

1. Dry fry the walnuts on a medium heat for 2 minutes or until a light browning appears. Remove from the heat and leave to cool.
2. Mix the olive oil and pomegranate molasses in a measuring jug, then leave to one side.
3. Combine the tomatoes, peppers, onion, parsley, garlic, and walnuts in a large mixing bowl.
4. Sprinkle the sumac evenly over the salad.
5. Pour the olive oil and molasses mix on top then mix thoroughly, ensuring all ingredients are coated.
6. Add lemon juice and salt to taste, then serve.

Chef's tips: Feta makes a welcome addition (non-vegan) to this dish, crumbled through the salad.

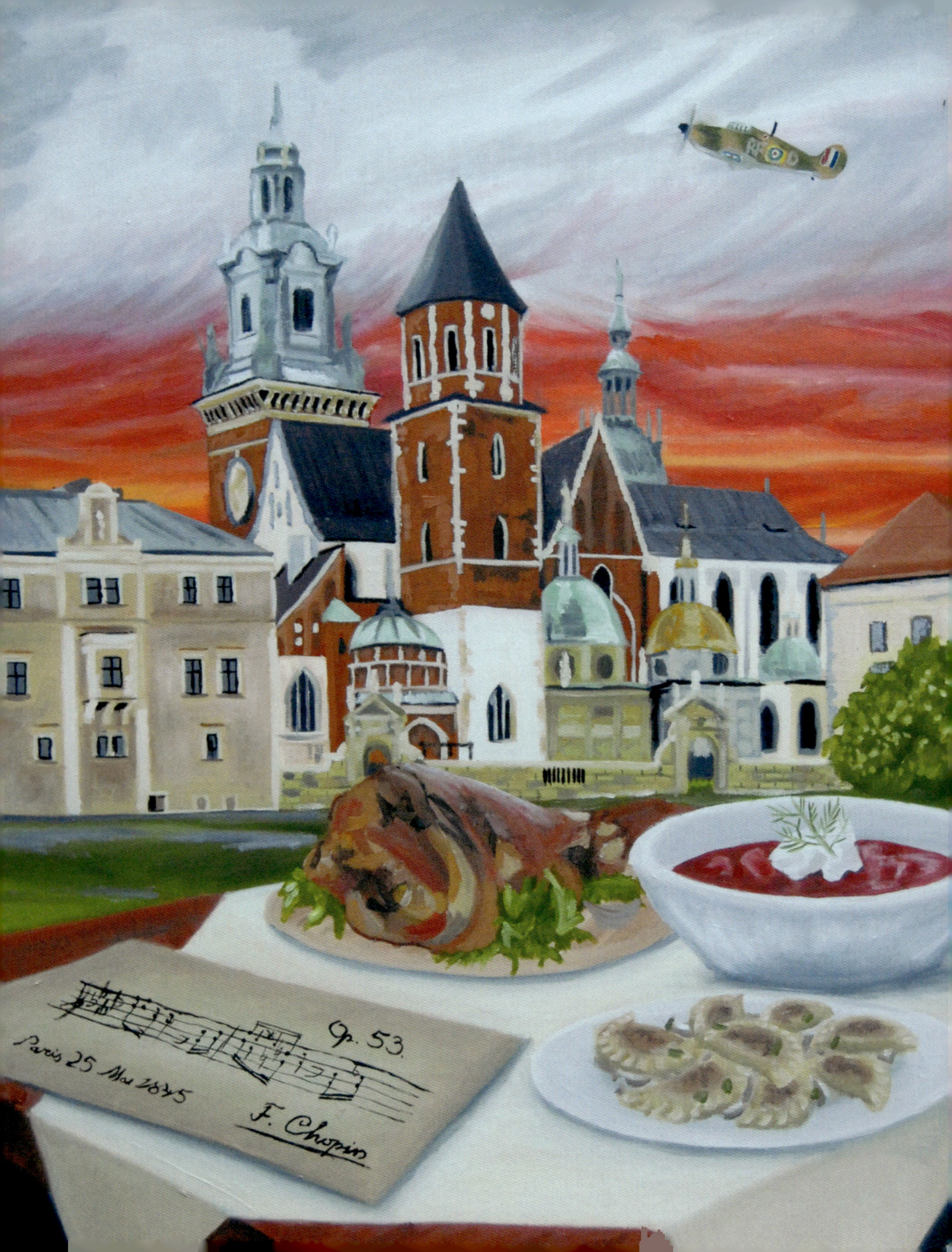
Op. 53.
Paris 25 Mai 1845
F. Chopin

POLAND

Art by Christian Turner

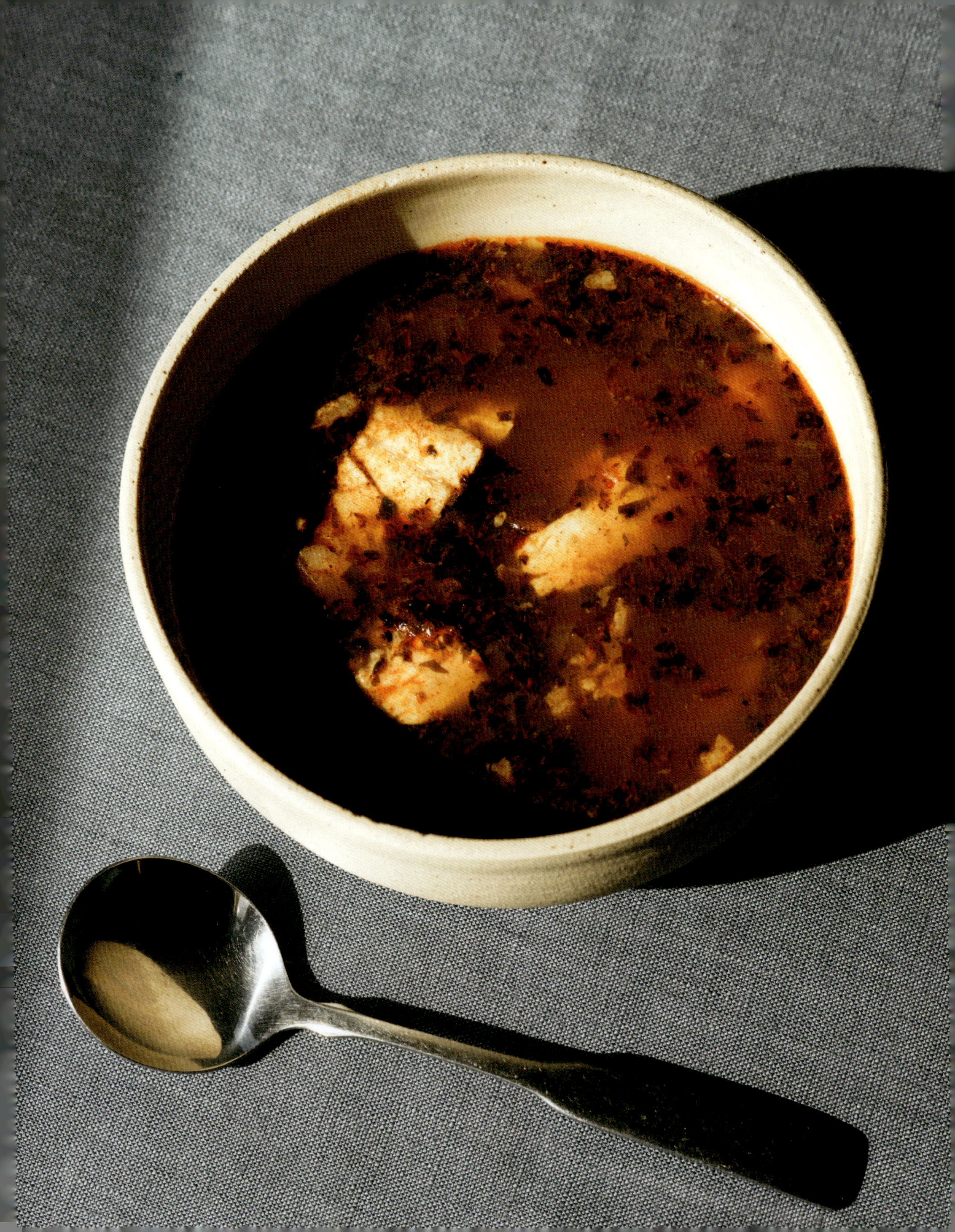

ZUPA RYBNA

Serves 4 | 60 mins

This hearty classic is perfect for an autumn evening.

INGREDIENTS

2 fillets of white fish of your choice, cut into chunks
2 sweet potatoes, peeled and diced
1 brown onion, sliced
2 sticks of celery, finely chopped
2 carrots, diced
2 handfuls of fresh parsley, finely chopped
3 garlic cloves, crushed
Handful of fresh thyme sprigs
Juice and zest of 2 lemons
3 tbsps balsamic vinegar
1 litre vegetable stock
2 tsps allspice
½ tsp ground nutmeg
1 tsp smoked paprika
1 tsp dried oregano
1 tbsp butter
2 tbsps vegetable oil
Salt and pepper to taste

METHOD

1. Add the vegetable oil to a large pan over a medium heat. Add the carrots and celery then fry until a slight browning appears.

2. Add the onions, balsamic vinegar and a pinch of salt. Once the onions begin to soften add the garlic, stirring throughout. Cook for a further 2 minutes.

3. Lower the heat then add the allspice, nutmeg, smoked paprika and oregano. Mix thoroughly, then raise the heat and cook for an extra minute, ensuring none of the spices stick to the bottom of the pan.

4. Add the stock, butter, sweet potatoes and thyme. Place a lid on the pan and cook for 25 minutes or until the potatoes are soft.

5. Add the parsley, lemon zest and juice.

6. Add the fish and poach on a simmer for 5 minutes or until cooked through.

Chef's tips: This is a fairly loose soup so serve with bread that can soak up the juices.
VEGAN SWITCH Use vegan butter, vegetable stock and pan-fried courgette instead of fish.

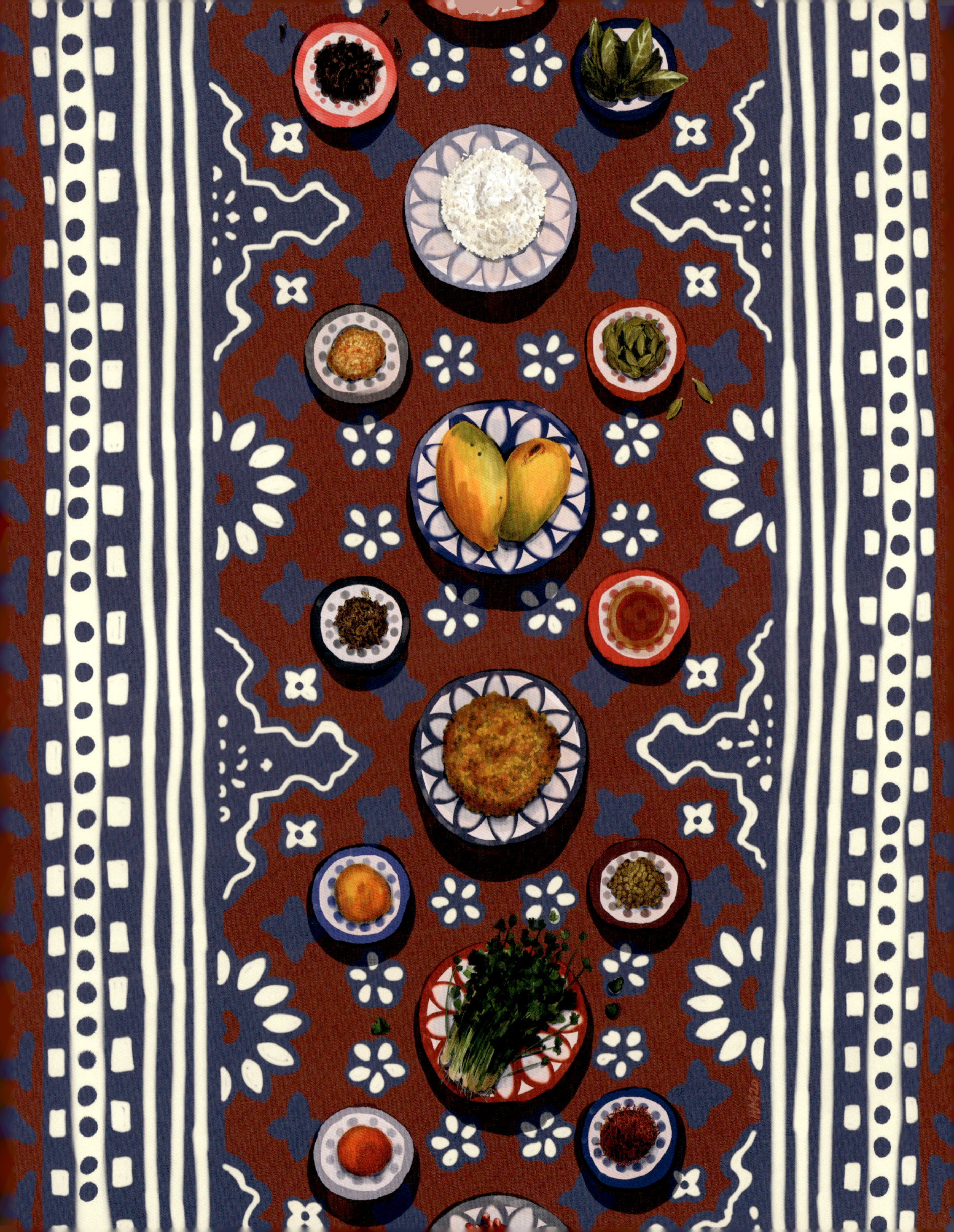

PAKISTAN

Art by Holly Gorne

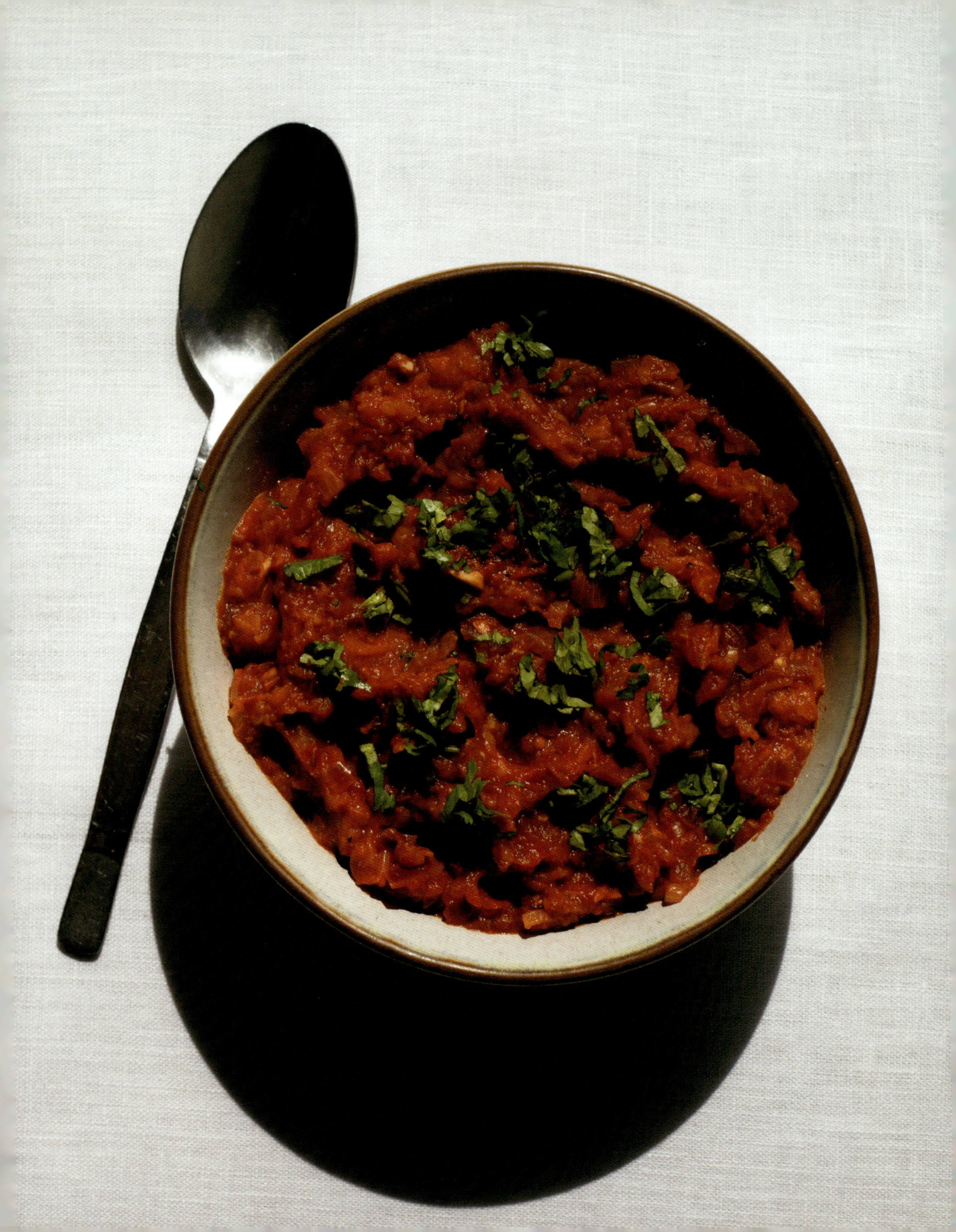

BAINGAN BHARTA

Serves 3-4 | 25 mins | Vegan

This traditional Pakistani curry is full of favour and showcases what you can do with an aubergine!

INGREDIENTS

1 tbsp vegetable oil
1 red onion, diced
1 green chilli, deseeded and finely chopped
400g tin of chopped tomatoes
2 garlic cloves, crushed
1 thumb sized piece of ginger, grated
1 medium aubergine, whole
1 tsp cumin seeds
½ tsp cayenne pepper
1 tsp ground turmeric
1 tsp coriander seeds
Salt and pepper to taste
Handful of fresh coriander, finely chopped (optional)
Basmati rice (optional)
Chapatis (optional)

METHOD

1. Place a pan over a medium heat and then dry fry the cumin and coriander seeds for 2 minutes stirring to ensure they do not burn. Remove from the heat and crush with a pestle and mortar and combine with the turmeric and cayenne.

2. Place the aubergine over an open flame and char the outside for 15 minutes, rotating regularly. If you do not have access to an open flame cook in the oven for 25 minutes at 200°C. Once cooked through, separate the skin from the aubergine and discard. Roughly chop what remains of the aubergine.

3. Add the vegetable oil to a large pan over a medium heat. Add the onion, with a pinch of salt and cook for 5 minutes, stirring throughout.

4. Next reduce to low heat and add the spice mix and cook for 2 minutes ensuring that nothing burns.

5. Now add the garlic, chilli, and ginger and cook for 2 minutes.

6. Add the chopped aubergine and tomatoes. Mix and cook for 10 minutes then serve.

Chef's tips
Add extra chillies if you want more heat!
Freshly chopped coriander works well as an optional garnish on top.
Serve with a chapati (see page 113) and/or basmati rice.

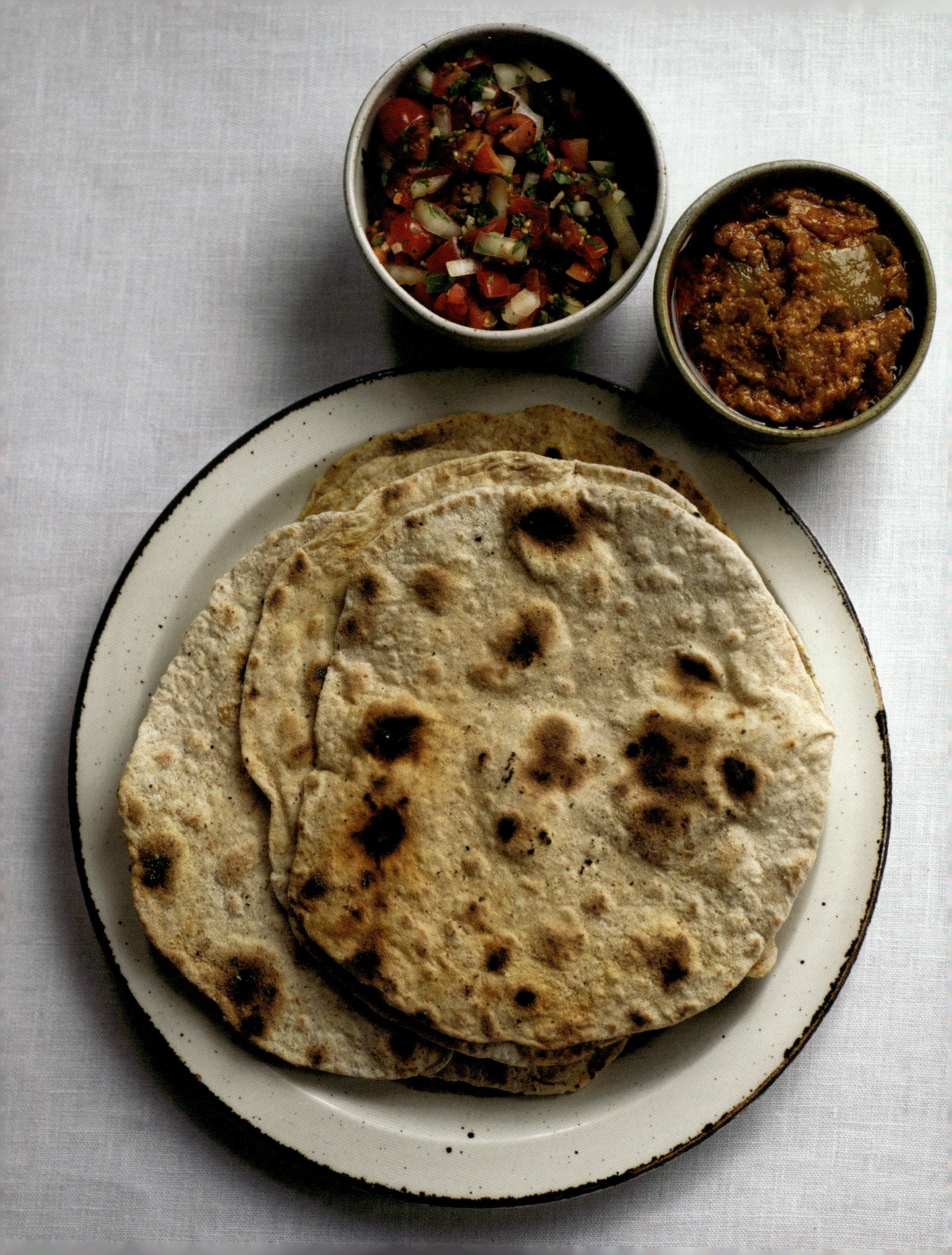

CHAPATIS

Serves 4 | 20 mins | Vegan

These flatbreads are a regular accompaniment to many Pakistani dishes. They are best cooked fresh and eaten straight away!

INGREDIENTS

125g chapati flour
2 tsps vegetable oil
½ tsp salt
125ml warm water

METHOD

1. Sieve the flour into a large mixing bowl. Add the salt.
2. Create a well in the flour. Add the vegetable oil then begin to add the water a little at a time, mixing with a fork at first then kneading by hand. You're aiming for a soft, elastic ball of dough.
3. Sprinkle a little flour onto a flat surface and continue the kneading process for at least 5 minutes, the longer you knead the softer the chapatis will be.
4. Divide the dough into 8 equally sized balls.
5. Flatten the balls slightly, then roll them out into a flat disc shape. Add flour to the flat surface and to the rolling pin as required during this process.
6. Heat a shallow frying pan. Lay the chapati on top and cook for 30 seconds or until the surface begins to bubble and lightly char.
7. Turn the chapati over with tongs and cook the other side in the same way.
8. Repeat with the other 7 discs. Cover completed chapatis with tin foil as you go to prevent them from drying out.

Chef's tips: Adding oil to your dough helps it stay soft and pliable and means you shouldn't need any extra in the frying pan. Use a tawa pan, if you have one, for even better results!

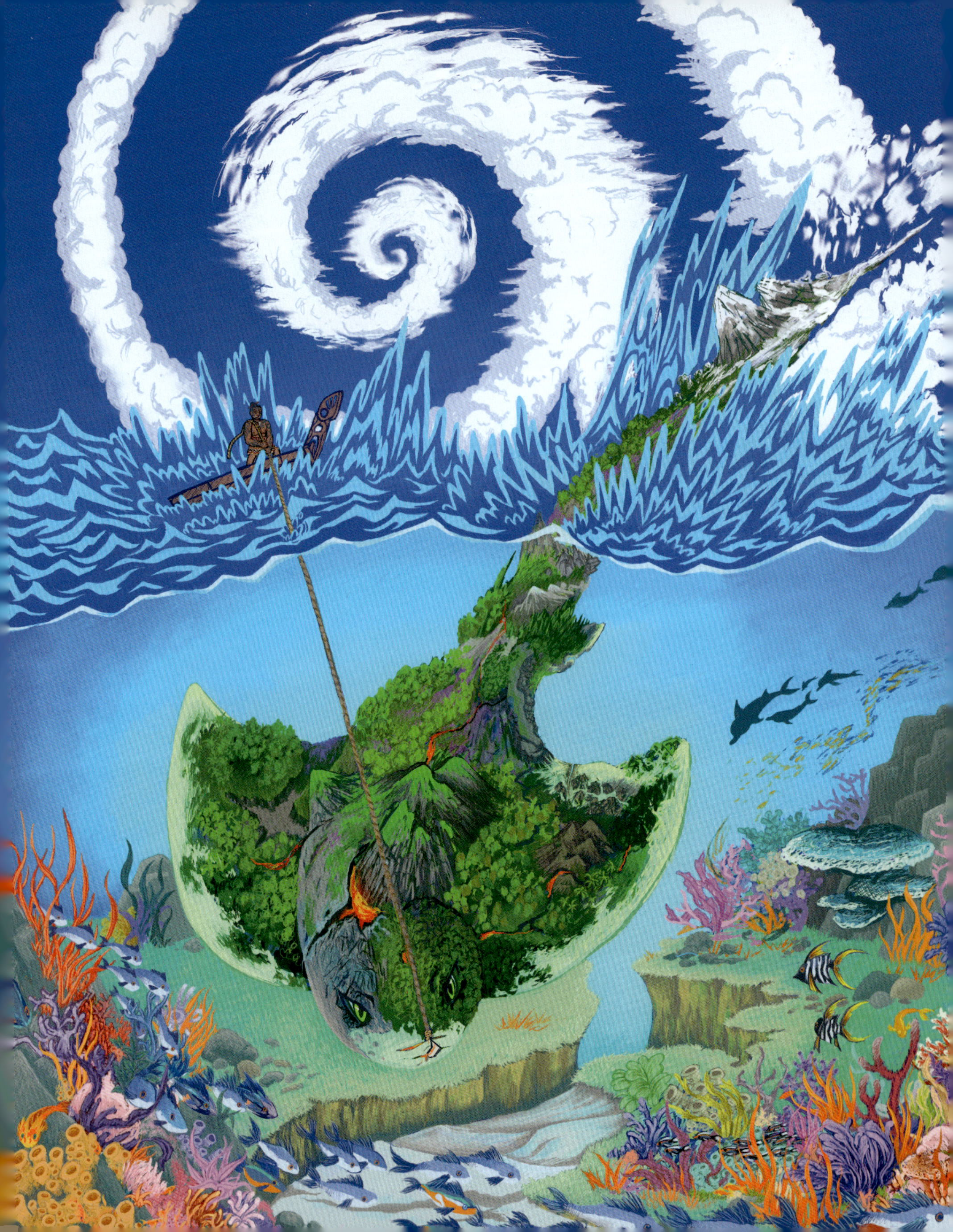

NEW ZEALAND

Art by Emily Gibbs

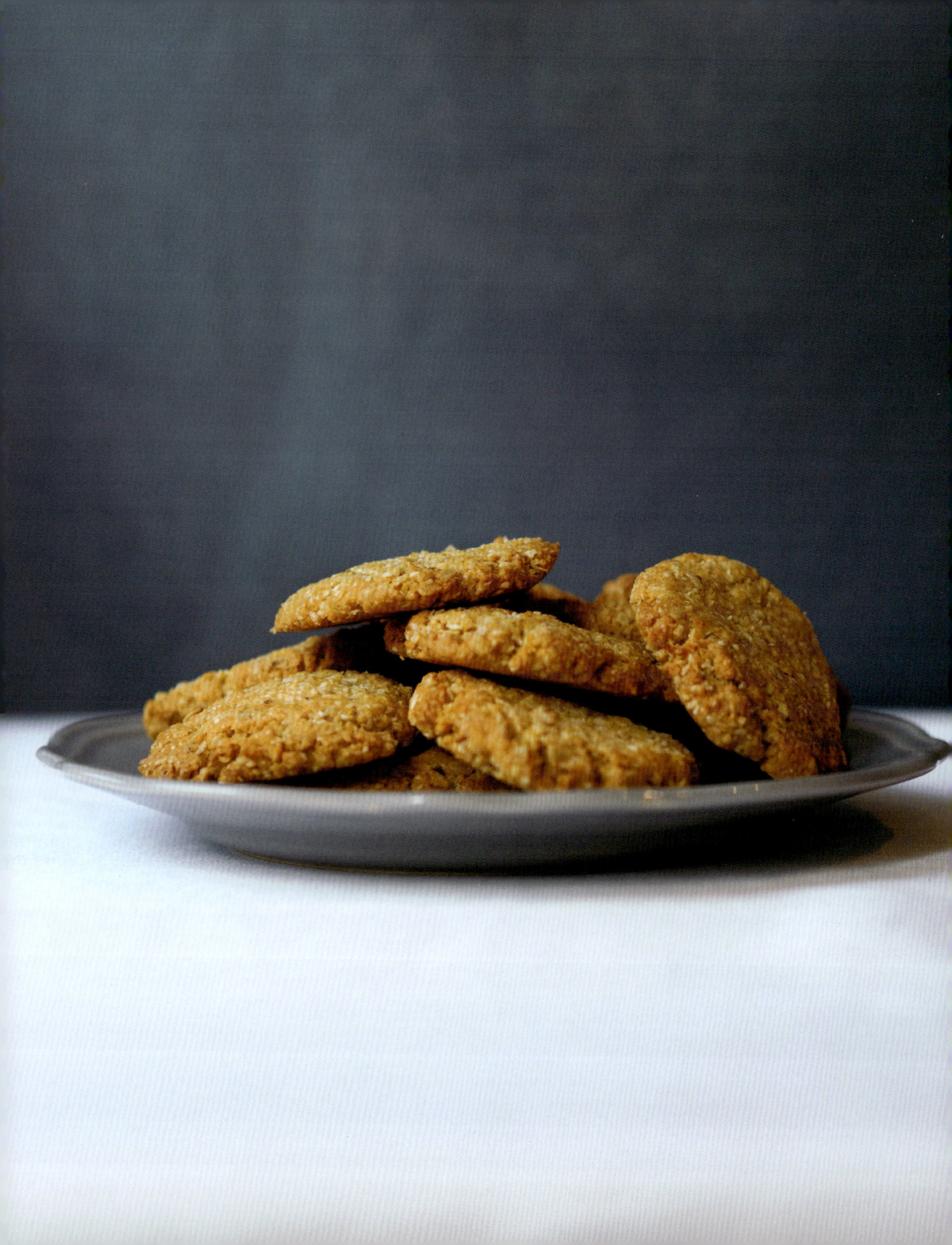

ANZAC BISCUITS

Serves 4-6 | **40 mins** | **Vegetarian**

Sweet coconut delights that perfectly accompany a cuppa.

INGREDIENTS

150g plain flour
100g desiccated coconut
150g sugar
120g oats
2 tbsps golden syrup
100g butter
½ tsp baking soda
2 tbsps boiling water

METHOD

1. Pre-heat the oven to 180°C. Prepare a baking tray with greaseproof paper brushed with butter.
2. Sieve the flour into a mixing bowl and combine with the sugar, oats and coconut. Leave to one side.
3. Add the butter and golden syrup to a pan and melt over a low heat.
4. Separately, mix together the baking soda and boiling water. Add this to the pan then take off the heat.
5. Form a well in the bowl with the dry ingredients, then slowly add the syrup mix until a thick, sticky dough is formed. Add more golden syrup to help bind if necessary.
6. Take a small amount of dough and roll into a ball. Flatten into a disc no larger than the palm of your hand.
7. Place all the discs on a baking tray and cook for 15 minutes or until golden brown.

Chef's tips

VEGAN SWITCH Simply use vegan butter instead!

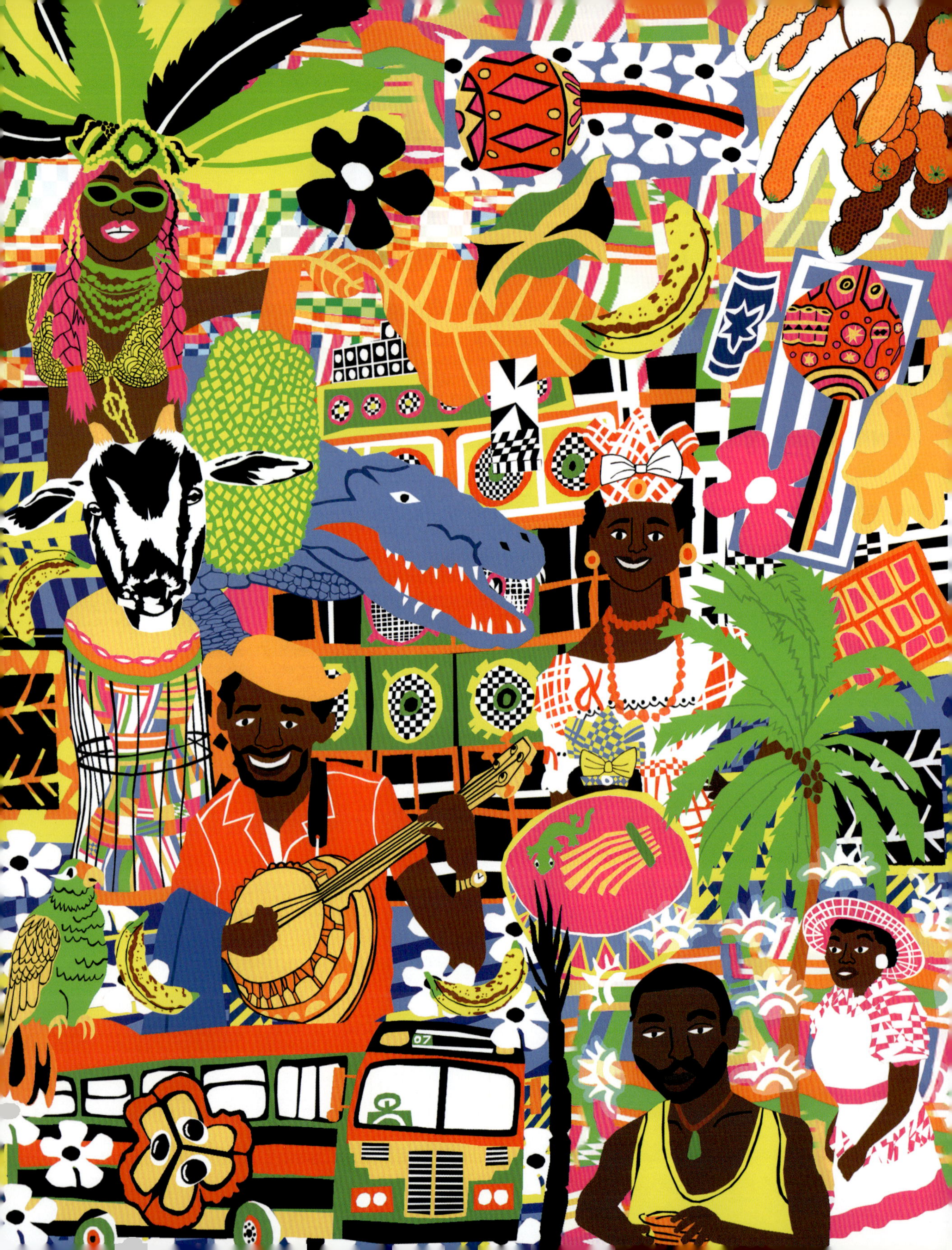
07

JAMAICA

Art by Amberley Garland

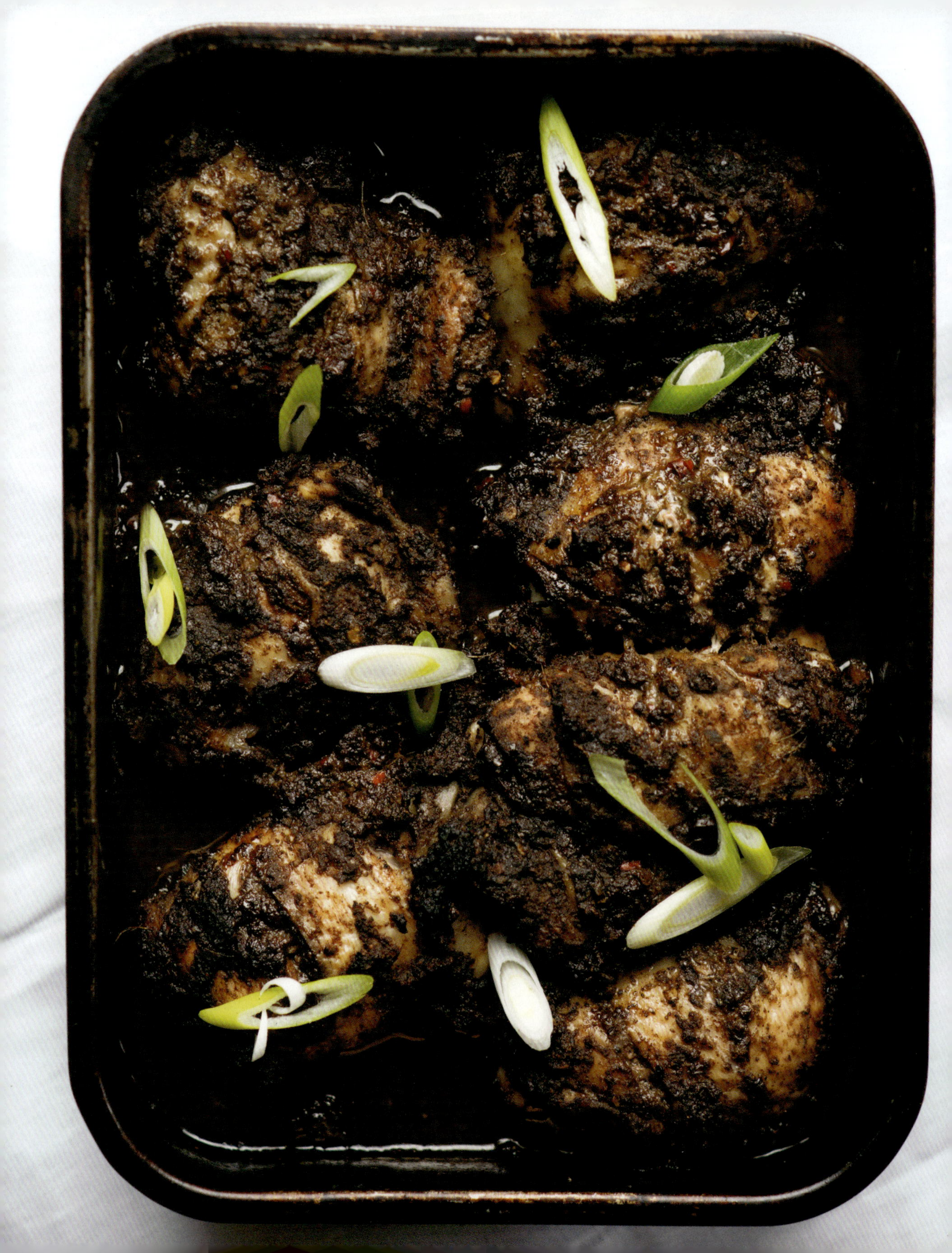

JERK CHICKEN WITH GRAVY

Serves 6 | 60 mins

This warm, aromatic dish is a real crowd-pleaser!

INGREDIENTS

1kg chicken thighs

FOR THE MARINADE

5 garlic cloves, crushed
3 scotch bonnet chillies
100g spring onions, sliced
Handful of fresh thyme leaves
1 thumb-sized piece of ginger, peeled and grated
4 tsps allspice
3 tsps of salt
1 tsp ground nutmeg
6 tbsps muscovado sugar
Juice of 2 lemons
1 brown onion, diced
2 tbsps olive oil

FOR THE GRAVY

700ml chicken stock
2 tbsps muscovado sugar
2 tbsps plain white flour
2 tbsps tomato ketchup

METHOD

1. Add all the marinade ingredients to a blender and blitz until the the mixture has an even consistency. Remove 3 tablespoons of marinade and leave in a small container in the fridge.

2. Place the chicken thighs in a large mixing bowl then coat them with the remaining marinade. Cover the bowl with cling film and leave in the fridge for 1 hour.

3. Pre-heat the oven to 200°C. Arrange the chicken in an oven tray, cover with tin foil then cook for 25 minutes.

4. Prepare the gravy while the chicken cooks. Add the chicken stock to a large pan over a medium heat then mix in the spare marinade that was left in the fridge, muscovado sugar and tomato ketchup.

5. Sieve the flour into a small container, gradually adding water until the flour has dissolved. Add this to the gravy and stir, ensuring no clumps appear. Keep the gravy warm on a low heat.

6. Remove the tin foil from the chicken after it has had 30 minutes in the oven. Cook for a further 15 minutes or until the juices run clear, then serve with the gravy.

Chef's tips

Scotch bonnet chillies give this dish its signature flavour but use a milder variety if you're averse to heat. Sometimes dark soy sauce is used in the marinade for an extra sticky glaze. Try barbequing the chicken on a sunny day.
VEGAN SWITCH Replace the chicken thighs with a cauliflower, apply marinade and roast instead. Use vegan-friendly vegetable stock in the gravy!

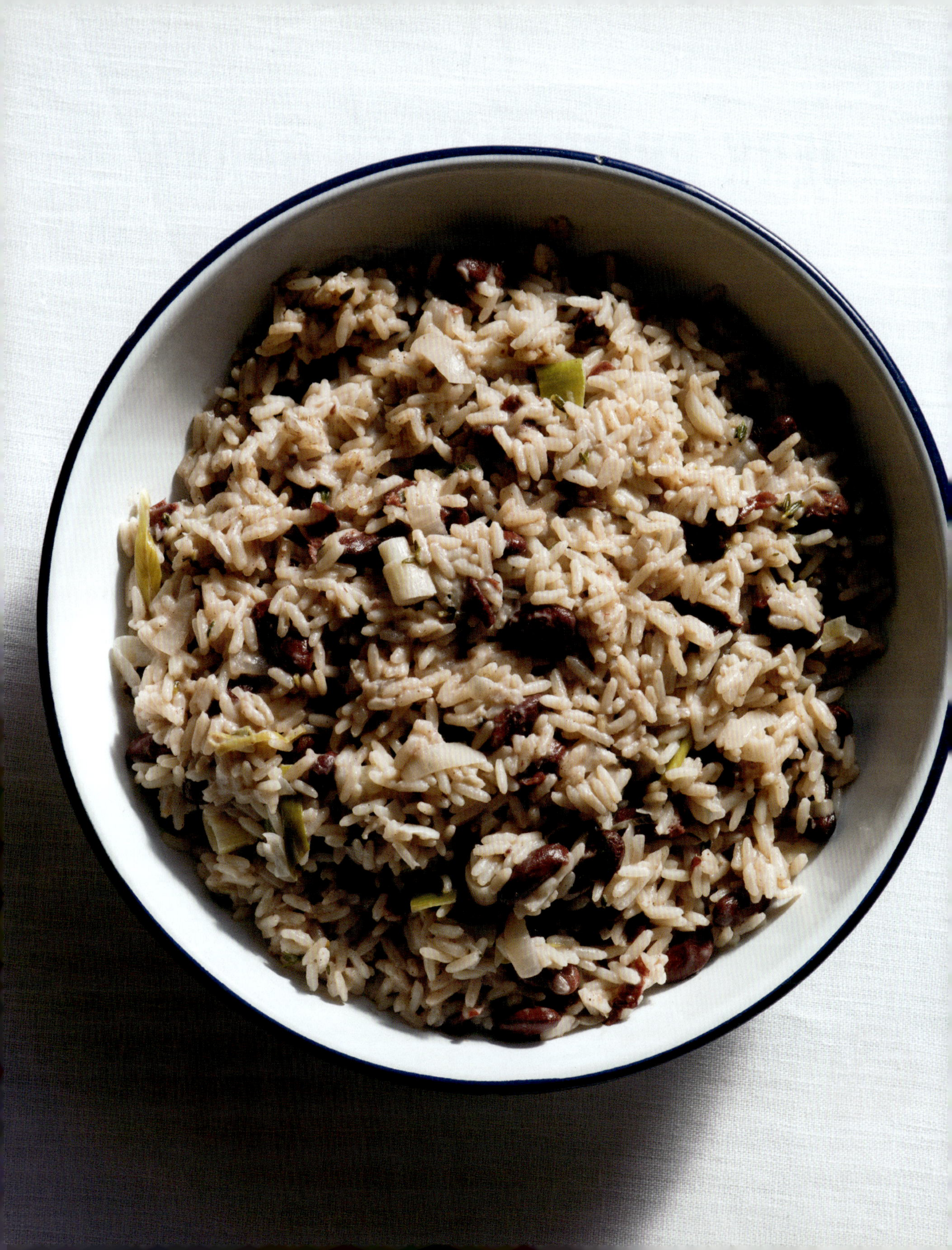

RICE & PEAS

Serves 6 | **40 mins** | **Vegetarian**

This staple rice dish is full of rich, warm flavours.

INGREDIENTS

300g basmati rice, washed
1 brown onion, diced
60g spring onions, sliced
400ml tin of coconut milk
400g tin of kidney beans, drained and rinsed
3 tbsps thyme leaves
3 garlic cloves, crushed
2 tbsps butter
2 tsps allspice
100ml of water
Salt to taste
1 scotch bonnet chilli (optional)

METHOD

1. Melt the butter in a large pan over a medium heat. Add the onions and a pinch of salt then cook for 5 minutes or until soft.
2. Add the garlic and spring onions then cook for a further 2 minutes.
3. Lower the heat then add the allspice, thyme, coconut milk, water, kidney beans and rice.
4. Bring to the boil then place a lid on the pan. Reduce to a low heat and cook for 20 minutes. Loosen with a dash of water if required.

Chef's tips
Add a whole, uncut scotch bonnet chilli for an extra kick of heat!
VEGAN SWITCH Use vegan butter or fry the onions in vegetable oil instead.

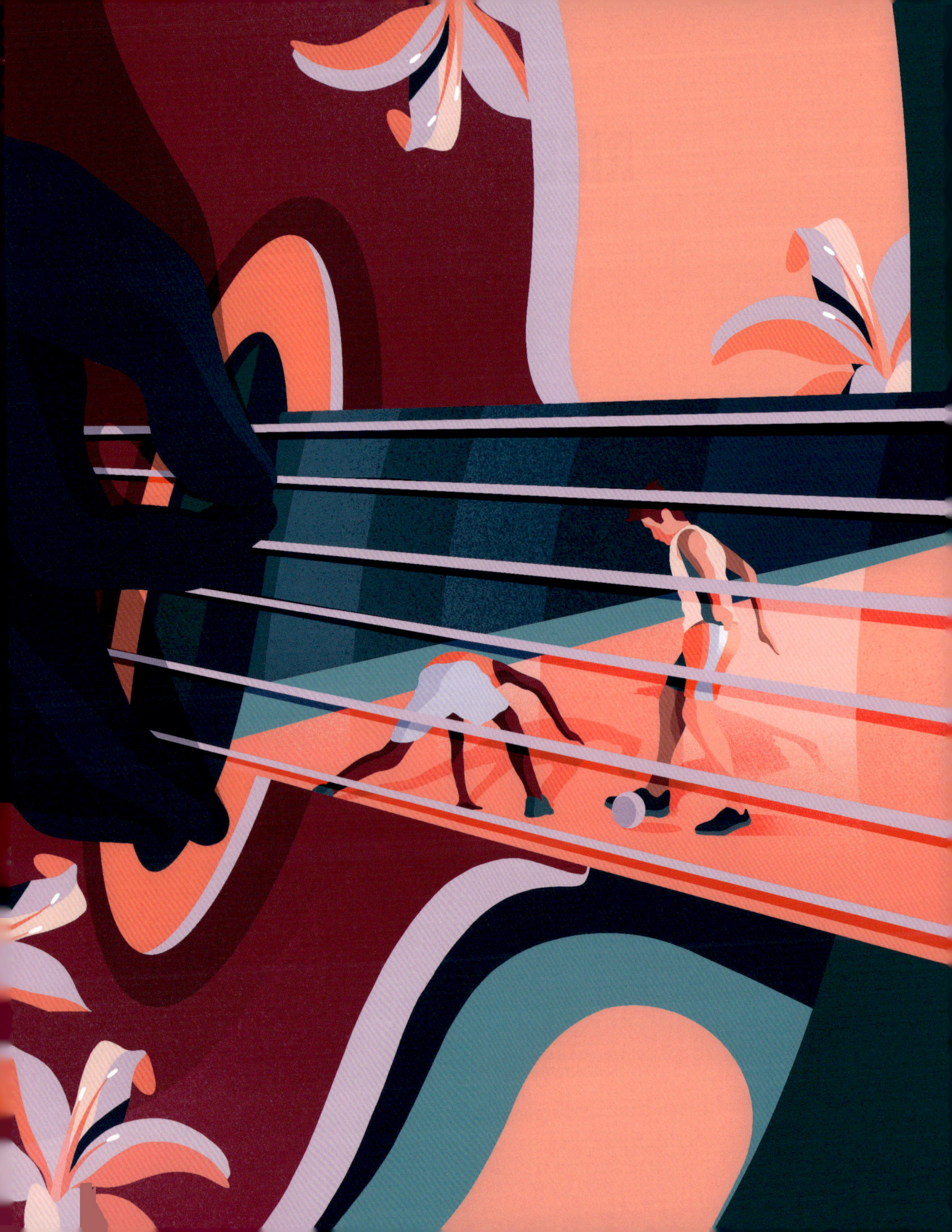

CUBA

Art by Ollie Hirst

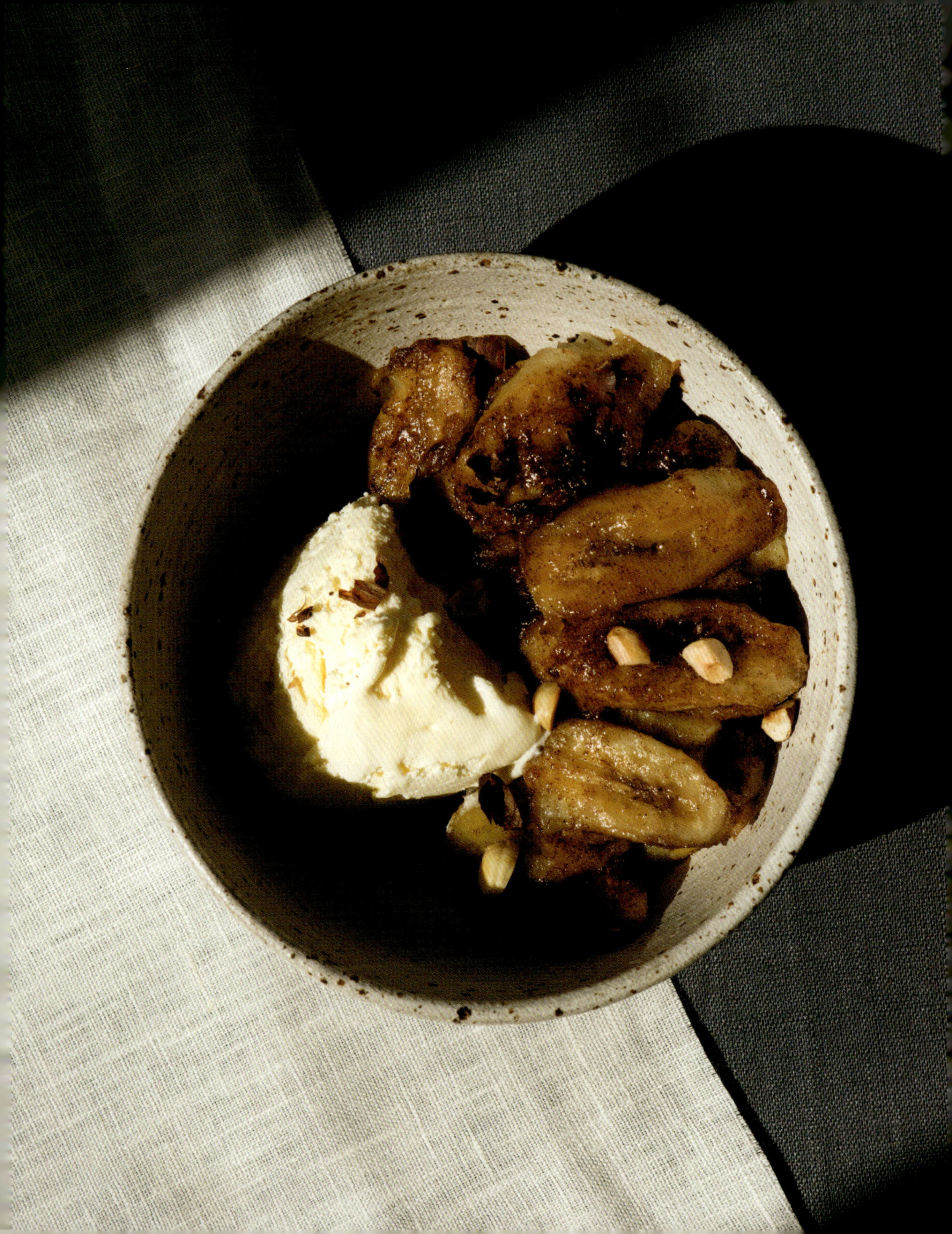

BAKED BANANAS

Serves 6 | **30 mins** | **Vegetarian**

This simple Cuban dessert is an irresistible classic!

INGREDIENTS

6 bananas, cut into large chunks
50g butter
5 tbsps brown sugar
2 tsps ground cinnamon
Handful of hazelnuts, roughly chopped

METHOD

1. Pre-heat the oven to 180°C. Prepare a baking tray with greaseproof paper brushed with butter.
2. Combine the sugar and cinnamon in a mixing bowl.
3. Melt the butter in a pan over a medium heat, then fry the bananas until they are lightly brown.
4. Place the bananas on the oven tray and coat evenly with the sugar and cinnamon mix.
5. Cover the tray with tin foil then cook in the oven for 10 minutes or until the sugar has melted. Top with nuts and serve.

Chef's tips

Serve with vanilla ice cream on a hot summer's day.
VEGAN SWITCH Use vegan butter and dairy free ice cream.

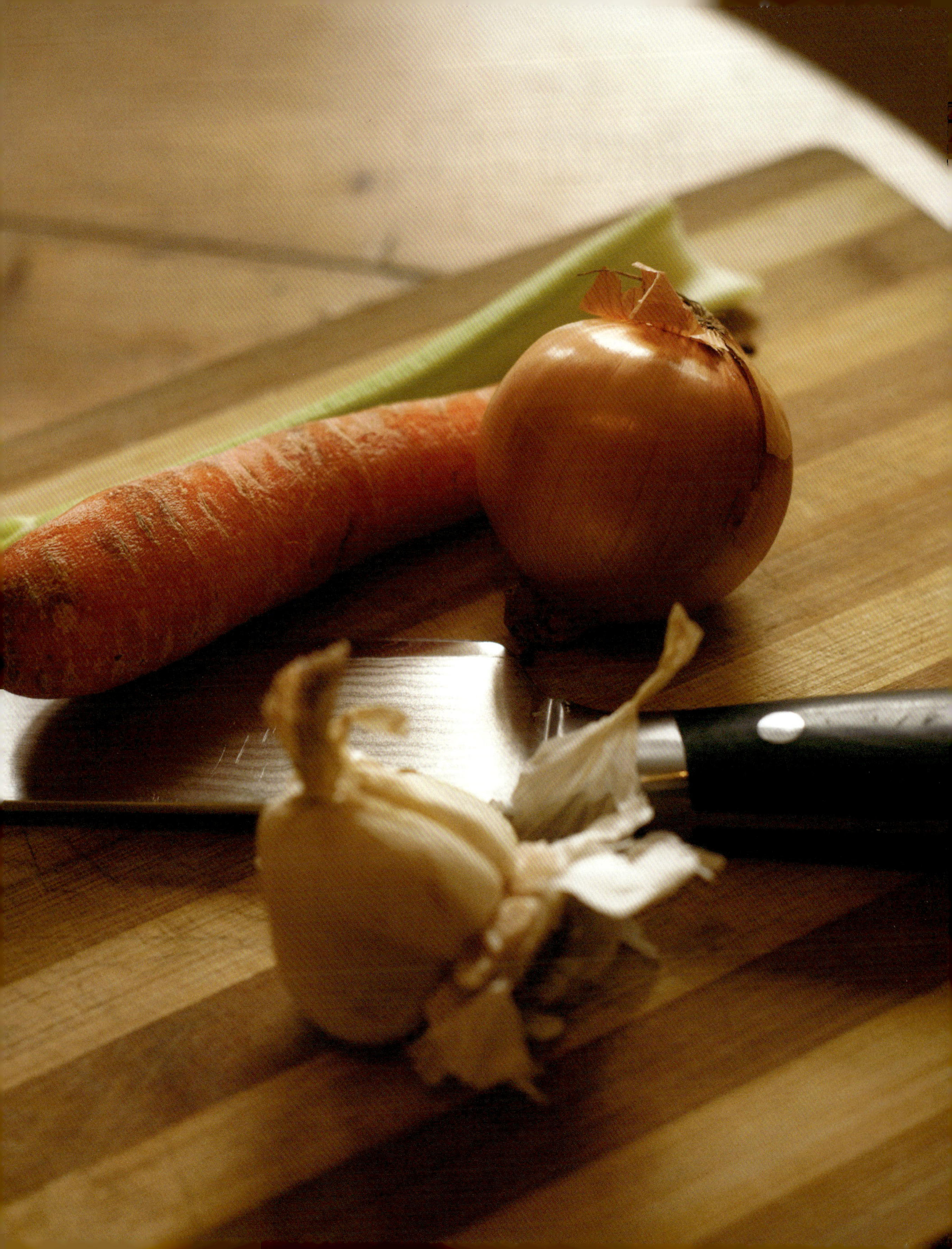

STOCKS

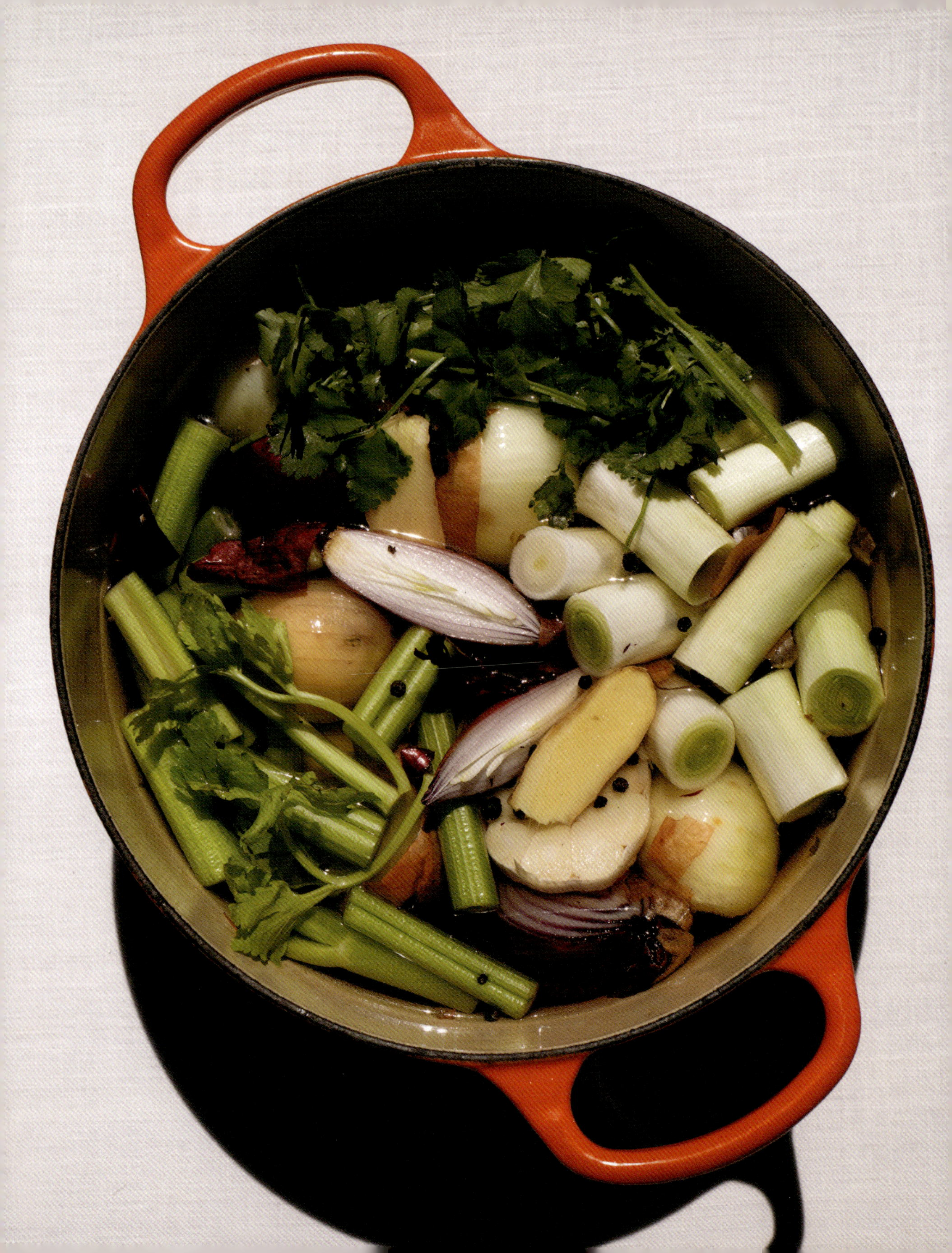

CHICKEN STOCK

Serves 3-4 | **180 mins**

This versatile stock can be used as the base for a variety of soups and is full of flavour!

INGREDIENTS

3 litres water
1 chicken carcass
2 celery sticks, roughly chopped
2 carrots, roughly chopped
2 brown onions, halved with skin on
3 garlic cloves, halved
Handful of fresh rosemary
Handful of fresh thyme
½ tbsp of black peppercorns, whole

METHOD

1. Add the oil to a large pan over a medium heat. Fry the onions, carrots and celery sticks until they are slightly browned.
2. Add the water and chicken carcass, bones and all. Bring to the boil, reduce to a medium heat and add all the other ingredients.
3. Cover with a lid and leave to reduce for 2½ hours.
4. Using a sieve, separate the liquid from the other ingredients. Discard the chicken remains and vegetables as they will be tasteless. Use your stock as required.

VEGETABLE STOCK

Serves 3-4 | **180 mins** | **Vegan**

This traditional stock is perfect for soup and gravy!

INGREDIENTS

3 litres water
3 celery sticks, roughly chopped
2 carrots, roughly chopped
2 brown onions, halved with skin on
4 garlic cloves, halved
Handful of fresh rosemary
Handful of fresh thyme
1 tbsp of black peppercorns, whole

METHOD

1. Add the oil to a large pan over a medium heat. Fry the onions, carrots and celery sticks until they are slightly browned.
2. Add the water and bring to the boil. Reduce to a medium heat and add all the other ingredients.
3. Cover with a lid and leave to reduce for 2½ hours.
4. Using a sieve, separate the liquid from the other ingredients. Discard the vegetable remains as they will be tasteless. Use your stock as required.

Chef's tips

Leave the skins on the onions for extra colour.
Add extra herbs to create your own signature stock.

mighty oaks **FROM LITTLE** *acorns grow*

Bounceback Food CIC began life in 2014, when we first tested the **buy one, give one** concept with a basic range of food at a Christmas market stall in Salford. It quickly became clear that as well as our foodbank drive, we would need to be able to teach people how to cook in order to tackle food poverty effectively.

Applying the **buy one, give one** model to our public cookery courses gave us a way of self-funding the social impact we set out to achieve and brought people from all walks of life together through food. Celebrating the diversity of different cultures and ensuring that everyone in the community is welcome to attend, has helped us to build a community cookery school that has proudly supported people in Greater Manchester, Cheshire and North Wales for over 6 years.

We now have a sustainable model that we're ready to share via social franchising. Over the next few years this will enable us to scale up our social impact across the UK and around the world! Visit our website (www.bouncebackfood.co.uk) for more details and follow our story on social media to see how we're getting on.

Once again, thank you for supporting the development of our community cookery school and hopefully we'll see you soon!

Much love,

The Bounceback Team

Bounceback Food @BouncebackFood BouncebackFood

INDEX

A
Aji amarillo paste	47
Allspice	63, 107, 121, 123
Almond milk	51, 71
Arborio rice	41
Aubergine	47, 111
Avocado	53

B
Baking soda	117
Balsamic vinegar	107
Banana	127
Basil	43
Beef steak	47
Black peppercorns	59, 131
Bread	37, 63, 67, 101, 107
Breadcrumbs	31, 71
Brown onion	41, 51, 59, 63, 71, 77, 81, 91, 93, 97, 107, 121, 123, 131
Brown sugar	127
Butter	67, 71, 101, 107, 117, 123, 127

C
Capers	43
Cardamom pods	59, 63
Carrot	107, 131
Cauliflower	121
Cayenne pepper	63, 77, 111
Celery	107, 131
Chapati flour	113
Cheddar cheese	71
Chicken carcass	131
Chicken stock	51, 63, 121, 131
Chicken thighs	121
Chickpeas	37, 63
Chilli flakes	53, 81, 91, 101
Chilli powder	37
Chilli sauce	47
Chillies	57, 59, 67, 73, 77, 87, 111, 121
Chinese five spice	91
Chips	47
Cinnamon, ground	59, 63, 127
Cinnamon stick	81
Cloves	59
Coconut	117
Coconut milk	59, 81, 83, 123
Coriander	47, 51, 53, 59, 73, 77, 81, 87, 111
Coriander seeds	59, 63, 81, 111
Courgette	107
Crudités	53
Cucumber	33, 57, 93, 103
Cumin, ground	31, 37, 47, 77
Cumin seeds	63, 111
Curry leaves	81

D
Dairy free ice cream	127
Desiccated coconut	117
Dried chillies	59

E
Egg	37, 71, 83, 91, 101

F
Fennel seeds	59
Fenugreek, ground	63, 81
Feta cheese	103
Fish sauce	59
Flour	71, 83, 117, 121

G
Garlic	31, 37, 41, 43, 47, 51, 59, 63, 67, 77, 81, 87, 91, 97, 101, 103, 107, 111, 121, 123, 131
Ginger	59, 63, 77, 91, 97, 111, 121
Golden syrup	117
Greek yoghurt	101
Green beans	97
Green chillies	77, 87, 111
Green pepper	103

H
Hazelnuts	127

I
Ice cream	127

J
Jalapeño	51

K
Kidney beans	63, 123

L
Lemon	31, 33, 43, 67, 87, 97, 103, 107, 121
Lemongrass	59
Lentils	63
Lettuce	33
Light soy sauce	47, 91, 97
Lime	51, 53, 59, 73, 81
Long grain rice	51

M
Macaroni	71
Malt vinegar	101
Milk	51, 71
Mint	33
Miso paste	91
Muscovado sugar	121

N
Noodles	91
Nutmeg, ground	63, 107, 121

O

Oat milk	51, 71
Oats	117
Oil	31, 33, 37, 41, 43, 47, 51, 63, 67, 71, 77, 81, 87, 91, 97, 101, 103, 107, 111, 113, 123, 121
Olive oil	31, 33, 37, 41, 43, 51, 63, 67, 71, 87, 101, 103, 121
Onion	37, 41, 47, 51, 53, 57, 59, 63, 71, 77, 81, 91, 93, 97, 103, 107, 111, 121, 123, 131
Oregano	47, 87, 107
Oyster sauce	97

P

Pak choi	91
Palm sugar	59
Paprika	37, 47, 63, 67, 71, 107
Parmesan	41, 43
Parsley	33, 37, 67, 71, 87, 101, 103, 107
Peanuts	59
Peanut butter	77
Pepper	37, 43, 47, 59, 63, 107, 111, 131
Peppercorns	59, 131
Peppers	31, 37, 47, 97, 103
Pesto	41, 43
Pineapple	73
Pine nuts	43
Pitta bread	33
Plain flour	71, 117, 121
Plant-based yoghurt	101
Pomegranate molasses	31, 103
Pomegranate seeds	103
Potato	59, 77, 107
Prawns	67

R

Radish	33
Ramen noodles	91
Red chillies	57, 67, 73, 93, 97
Red lentils	63
Red onion	37, 47, 53, 57, 59, 91, 111
Red pepper	31, 37
Red wine vinegar	97
Rice	47, 51, 59, 97, 111, 123
Rice flour	83
Rice vinegar	57, 93
Rosemary	41, 131

S

Salt	31, 33, 37, 41, 43, 47, 53, 57, 59, 67, 71, 81, 93, 97, 101, 103, 107, 111, 113, 121, 123
Scotch bonnet chillies	47, 121, 123
Sesame oil	91, 97
Sesame seeds	91, 93
Smoked paprika	37, 47, 67, 71, 107
Soy sauce	47, 91, 97
Spinach	43, 51
Spring greens	77
Spring onions	33, 57, 59, 91, 97, 121, 123
Squid	97
Star anise	81
Stock	41, 51, 63, 77, 91, 107, 121, 131
Sugar	57, 59, 83, 93, 117, 121, 127
Sumac	33, 103
Sweet potato	77, 107
Syrup	117

T

Tamarind sauce	59
Thyme	31, 107, 121, 123, 131
Tiger prawns	67
Tinned chickpeas	37, 63
Tinned kidney beans	63, 123
Tinned tomatoes	37, 63, 111
Tofu	37, 67
Tomato ketchup	121
Tomato purée	37, 63, 77
Tomatoes	33, 37, 47, 53, 63, 103, 111
Tortilla chips	53
Turmeric, ground	81, 111

V

Vanilla ice cream	127
Vegan butter	67, 71, 101, 107, 117, 123, 127
Vegan cheese	41, 71
Vegetable oil	47, 77, 81, 97, 107, 111, 113, 123
Vegetable stock	41, 51, 77, 91, 107

W

Walnuts	31, 101, 103
White fish	107
White onion	103
White wine vinegar	57

Y

Yeast	83
Yoghurt	63, 101

BOUNCEBACK FOOD